Slovenes in Michigan

DISCOVERING THE PEOPLES OF MICHIGAN

Russell M. Magnaghi, *Series Editor*
Arthur W. Helweg and Linwood H. Cousins, *Founding Editors*

Ethnicity in Michigan: Issues and People
Jack Glazier and Arthur W. Helweg

African Americans in Michigan
Lewis Walker, Benjamin C. Wilson, and Linwood H. Cousins

Albanians in Michigan
Frances Trix

Amish in Michigan
Gertrude Enders Huntington

Arab Americans in Michigan
Rosina J. Hassoun

Asian Indians in Michigan
Arthur W. Helweg

Belgians in Michigan
Bernard A. Cook

Chaldeans in Michigan
Mary C. Sengstock

Copts in Michigan
Eliot Dickinson

Cornish in Michigan
Russell M. Magnaghi

Danes and Icelanders in Michigan
Howard L. Nicholson, Anders J. Gillis, and Russell M. Magnaghi

Dutch in Michigan
Larry ten Harmsel

Finland-Swedes in Michigan
Mika Roinila

Finns in Michigan
Gary Kaunonen

French in Michigan
Russell M. Magnaghi

French Canadians in Michigan
John P. DuLong

Germans in Michigan
Jeremy W. Kilar

Greeks in Michigan
Stavros K. Frangos

Haitians in Michigan
Michael Largey

Hmong Americans in Michigan
Martha Aladjem Bloomfield

Hungarians in Michigan
Éva V. Huseby-Darvas

Irish in Michigan
Seamus P. Metress and Eileen K. Metress

Italians in Michigan
Russell M. Magnaghi

Jews in Michigan
Judith Levin Cantor

Latinos in Michigan
David A. Badillo

Latvians in Michigan
Silvija D. Meja

Lithuanians in Michigan
Marius K. Grazulis

Maltese in Michigan
Joseph M. Lubig

Mexicans and Mexican Americans in Michigan
Rudolph Valier Alvarado and Sonya Yvette Alvarado

Norwegians in Michigan
Clifford Davidson

Poles in Michigan
Dennis Badaczewski

Scandinavians in Michigan
Jeffrey W. Hancks

Scots in Michigan
Alan T. Forrester

Serbians in Michigan
Paul Lubotina

Slovenes in Michigan
James E. Seelye Jr.

South Slavs in Michigan
Daniel Cetinich

Swedes in Michigan
Rebecca J. Mead

Yankees in Michigan
Brian C. Wilson

Discovering the Peoples of Michigan is a series of publications examining the state's rich multicultural heritage. The series makes available an interesting, affordable, and varied collection of books that enables students and educated lay readers to explore Michigan's ethnic dynamics. A knowledge of the state's rapidly changing multicultural history has far-reaching implications for human relations, education, public policy, and planning. We believe that Discovering the Peoples of Michigan will enhance understanding of the unique contributions that diverse and often unrecognized communities have made to Michigan's history and culture.

Slovenes in Michigan

James E. Seelye Jr.

Michigan State University Press

East Lansing

⊗ The paper used in this publication meets the minimum requirements of ANSI/NISO Z39.48-1992 (R 1997) (Permanence of Paper).

Michigan State University Press
East Lansing, Michigan 48823-5245

Printed and bound in the United States of America.

26 25 24 23 22 21 20 19 18 17 1 2 3 4 5 6 7 8 9 10

LIBRARY OF CONGRESS CATALOGING-IN-PUBLICATION DATA
Names: Seelye, James E., author.
Title: Slovenes in Michigan / James E. Seelye Jr.
Description: East Lansing : Michigan State University Press, 2017. | Series: Discovering the peoples of Michigan | Includes bibliographical references and index.
Identifiers: LCCN 2016040840| ISBN 9781611862546 (pbk. : alk. paper) | ISBN 9781609175368 (pdf) | ISBN 9781628953053 (epub) | ISBN 9781628963052 (kindle)
Subjects: LCSH: Slovenian Americans—Michigan—History. | Slovenian Americans—Michigan—Social conditions. | Immigrants—Michigan—History. | Michigan—Ethnic relations. | Michigan—Social conditions.
Classification: LCC F575.S65 S44 2017 | DDC 305.8009774—dc23 LC record available at https://lccn.loc.gov/2016040840

Book and cover design by Charlie Sharp, Sharp Des!gns, East Lansing, MI.
Cover portrait of Frederic Baraga is the official oil painting commissioned at the time of his elevation to Bishop of the Diocese of Sault Ste. Marie and Marquette and is used courtesy of Tom Buchkoe.

Michigan State University Press is a member of the Green Press Initiative and is committed to developing and encouraging ecologically responsible publishing practices. For more information about the Green Press Initiative and the use of recycled paper in book publishing, please visit *www.greenpressinitiative.org.*

Visit Michigan State University Press at *www.msupress.org*

This book is dedicated to my father,
James Edward Seelye Sr.

Contents

Acknowledgments

Work on this project began in 2003. I was enrolled in history courses with Dr. Russell Magnaghi at Northern Michigan University, and I completed a research paper on Frederic Baraga and John H. Pitezel, a Methodist missionary. That work morphed into a career change. Until that point I wanted to be a high school history teacher, but diving into the archives at Northern Michigan University compelled me to understand and appreciate the power of history, and I decided to earn a PhD instead. Baraga and other missionaries in Michigan stayed with me through 2010 and were the subjects of my research at the University of Toledo. For that, I must first thank Russell Magnaghi and for the opportunity to add a volume to the series that he has so adequately shepherded through Michigan State University Press. Also, to Chet DeFonso at Northern Michigan University, my undergraduate advisor, without whom I truly would not be where I am today. I also want to thank David Prychitko for showing me the way all academics should conduct their lives both inside and outside of their home institutions.

Funding for this research has been provided by a number of organizations. I was fortunate enough to receive a research grant from the Van Pelt and Opie Libraries at Michigan Technological University to do research in their wonderful facility, and I am forever grateful for the help they gave me.

The staffs at the Clarke Historical Library, the Bishop Baraga Association, and the Archdiocese of Detroit Archives provided much material and assistance. Marcus Robyns and his staff at the Central Upper Peninsula and Northern Michigan University Archives, a place I am proud to have worked for, have been immeasurably helpful in this work, as was the assistance of two Grace H. Magnaghi Visiting Research Fellowships. Lenora McKeen of the Bishop Baraga Association provided timely assistance and put me in touch with Dr. John Vidmar, whose help has been above and beyond.

I need to thank my colleagues in the history department at Kent State University at Stark, Leslie Heaphy, Ralph Menning, and Lindsay Starkey. A special thanks goes to Lindsay, who not only helped me with some Latin translations but whose friendship, kindness, and ability to make me laugh has helped me stay sane and keep things in perspective. Tim Bogner and Ann Martinez—new friends who have been lifelong friends—are phenomenal. I would also be remiss if I did not thank Jayne Moneysmith for organizing, and the administration of Kent State University at Stark for supporting, the Writing Boot Camps, which served as endless sources of inspiration and motivation. In addition, Mike Roberto has proven to be a tireless source of support, as has my great friend Katie Baer, without whom I would be particularly lost. I also would like to extend my thanks Ashley Riley Sousa for everything, not the least of which, for making me remember to laugh often and hard and for reminding me to always move my goalposts, never be satisfied with the status quo, and keep striving for the best. I would also like to give monumental thanks to Julie Loehr of Michigan State University Press.

Speaking of perspective—when I first met Frederic Baraga, I had not met my wife, let alone been blessed with two beautiful children. Words cannot express my love and gratitude to my family for their help, support, and patience through this project, so I will simply say thank you. Emily, Abigail, and Audrey have made me love more than I ever thought was possible.

Finally, this work is dedicated to my father. His support over the years has been steadfast, much like the headaches, acid reflux, and stress that I have caused him. While I have edited two previous books, this is my first monograph, and I promised my dad that I would dedicate my first book to him, so here it is.

Any errors, misjudgments, or omissions are mine and mine alone. Even though countless people provided information and insights into this project, the end product is the result of my thoughts, writing, and synthesis. I have seen similar disclaimers in numerous works before, but until I completed this work, I never realized how true and important it is. Also, if I neglected to specifically thank you, know that you are not forgotten in my heart, and I will not forget that this work could not and would not have been completed without your guidance.

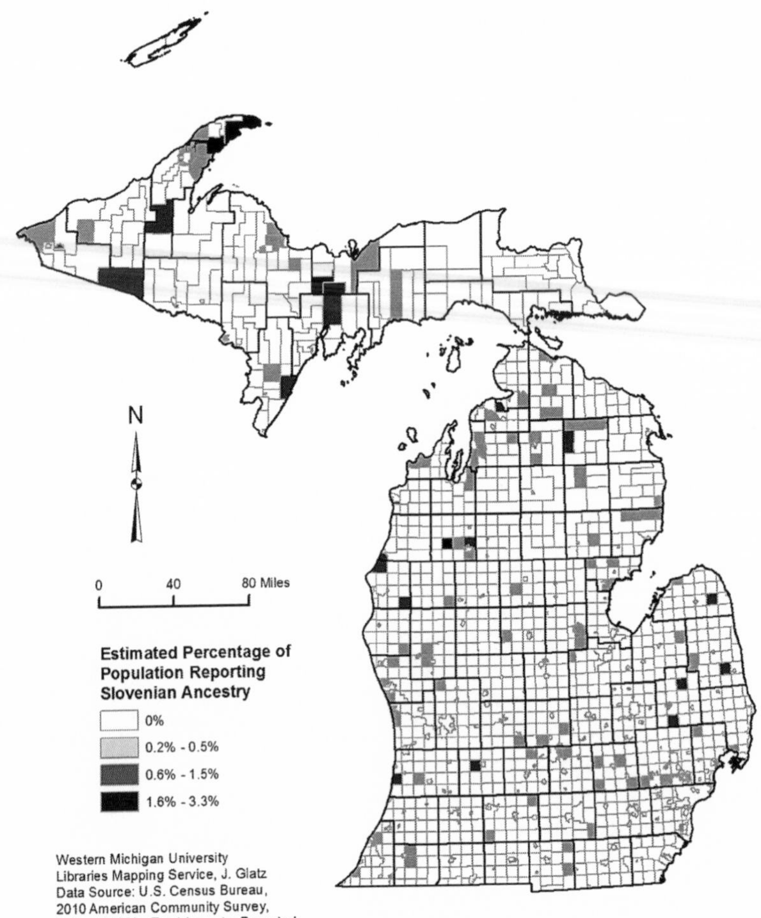
N
0
40
80 Miles
Estimated Percentage of Population Reporting Slovenian Ancestry
0%
0.2% - 0.5%
0.6% - 1.5%
1.6% - 3.3%
Western Michigan University
Libraries Mapping Service, J. Glatz
Data Source: U.S. Census Bureau,
2010 American Community Survey,
Table B04003 - Total Ancestry Reported

Introduction

Many citizens of Michigan are familiar with the name Frederic Baraga. They generally know that he was a missionary and a Catholic Bishop. He was also a Slovene. Baraga, along with Ignatius Mrak, John Vertin, and the Vertin brothers, illustrate the apotheosis of Slovenes in Michigan, but they made up a fragment of a relatively small number of South Slavs who started emigrating from Europe in the middle of the nineteenth century. Their numbers were never as vast as the Finns, Swedes, or Italians, but they made a cultural impact that is still felt today.

The story of the Slovenes in Michigan tends to be relegated to that of Frederic Baraga. There is more to the story. By taking the Slovene immigrant experience in Michigan as part of a greater pattern of immigration history, familiar themes emerge. Many Slovenes came to America with hopes of making enough money to travel back home in a much better financial situation, but the majority of them did not fulfill that dream. Slovenes tenaciously held onto their cultural heritage and ensured that traditions from home were not lost in the journey across the Atlantic. With the perpetuation of many of these traditions into the twenty-first century, the Slovenes' experience causes us to reconsider just how well the melting pot of the United States succeeded in acculturating immigrants. The plurality of ethnicities that make

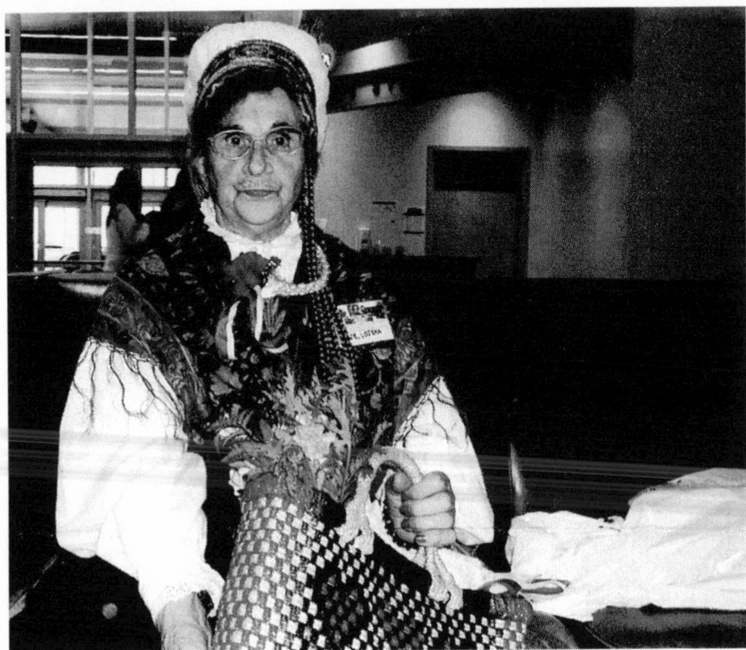

This woman is wearing traditional Slovene clothing at a Bishop Baraga Days celebration in Marquette. Credit: Tom Buchkoe and the Bishop Baraga Association, Marquette, MI.

up the United States only enriches our history and experience, and cultural differences need to be embraced.

Studying the Slovene experience in Michigan is not an easy undertaking. There is a paucity of sources on most Slovenes, with the exception of Baraga. However, since they were such an incredibly religious people, information can be found in church records. There were large communities in the Copper Country and in Detroit, and adequate records exist to tell those stories. While other smaller pockets of Slovenes were scattered throughout the state, their records were difficult, if not impossible, to locate. The issue is compounded by the interesting, diverse, and divisive history of Slovenia itself. It has not existed as in independent state for the majority of its long history, and most Slovenes identified themselves as Austrians to American governmental sources.

Historical Sketch of Slovenia

Today Slovenia encompasses nearly 7,896 square miles and is half the size of the Upper Peninsula. Approximately two-thirds of the country is comprised of the Alps, while the eastern third declines onto the Plains of Pannonia. Italy lies to the west, Austria to the north, Hungary to the east, and Croatia to the south. The population is slightly more than two million, and the capital is Ljubljana as the capital.

Archaeologists have discovered evidence of human habitation in the area that is now Slovenia that dates back to 250,000 years. Furthermore, the ruins of 4,500 year-old dwellings were found near Ljubljana in 2002. Two thousand years ago, the Roman Empire established a post known as Emona in present-day Ljubljana.

By around 1200, Slovenia was part of the Holy Roman Empire, although the empire was decentralized and weak. In the early sixteenth century, many ethnicities were under the Hungarian Empire, including Croats, Czechs, Germans, Italians, Magyars, Poles, Romanians, Serbs, Slovaks, and Slovenes. Virtually all Slovene lands were under the Hungarian Empire as well, including Styria, Carniola, and Carinthia. One of the empire's primary concerns was defending against Turkish invasions. At one point in the sixteenth century, the border of the Ottoman Empire advanced to within about nine miles of Slovene lands, and they experienced an average of five Turkish incursions each year.[1]

Estates and diets were divided into four groups that governed the Slovene peoples: prelates, higher nobility, lower nobility, and the towns. Towns had to fight for their right to participate in diets, and higher levels of governance controlled the administration of their lands.

Religion was central to Slovenes' lives. While many remained firmly attached to Catholicism, the Protestant Reformation made serious inroads and was widely adopted. Religious services were conducted in the vernacular, which consisted primarily of Slovene in Carniola and German in Styria and Carinthia. However, by the late sixteenth century, the Counter-Reformation was quite successful, and Protestantism was suppressed, with many clergy members forced to leave their towns. Depending upon both the ruler of the empire and the location within the empire, the level of suppression varied.

As a result of the constant threat of Turkish invasions, the tax burden increased throughout the sixteenth century, which, due to the prevailing way of governance, was felt particularly hard by peasants. Their economy was mainly agricultural, with some manufactured goods, including cloth, boots, gunpowder, beekeeping, and wax making. Furthermore, mining and iron smelting developed during this time period—skills that served the Slovene immigrants in Michigan incredibly well in the nineteenth century. There were also developments in mercury and copper, and cannonball production and gun-making foundries increased. Even with these advances, the economy stalled as trade was heavily disrupted by Turkish activity in Hungary and Croatia. As time progressed, tariffs increased, and the rights of peasants to migrate were restricted.

The Counter-Reformation continued to prevail in Slovenia as the sixteenth century passed into the seventeenth century. Absolutism took root gradually as well. In 1628, the nobility were ordered to either return to Catholicism or face exile. Some converted, but many simply left, immigrating to Hungary and Southern Germanic lands.

By 1631, the Bishop of Ljubljana wrote that the Slovene language was the rule among commoners, while those in authority spoke German, and the language of the educated was Italian. Prior to that, in 1615, printing of Slovene literature ceased. Most elementary schools used German, though some taught lessons in Italian. Slovene was used a small amount in religious instruction.[2]

From the mid-eighteenth to the mid-nineteenth century, the economy shifted somewhat. New crop production emerged that included buckwheat, corn, and millet. Cattle, sheep, and hogs were raised, although poultry was predominant. Mining, smelting, and copper work continued as well. Then there were governmental shifts, and around 1740 the estates started to lose control. During Maria Theresa's reign (1740–80), educational reforms took place. She ordered that elementary schools be established in every parish, with lower secondary schools in every major town and teacher colleges in the capital of each region. The use of the Slovene language increased, and measures were taken to improve the lives and conditions of the lower classes. These measures helped to build a larger Slovene national consciousness, but local entrenchments inhibited that as well. Different regions even identified themselves as different brands of Slovene. An illustration of that occurred between 1758–62, when a Catechism was printed in three different Slovene versions based on the region—Styria, Carinthia, and Carniola.

Many of these minor schisms ended with the emergence of nationalism and the resulting rising national consciousness of the late eighteenth and early nineteenth century, which was influenced by the Napoleonic Wars influenced this. The national awakening of Slovenia occurred slowly but steadily. Vienna, the governmental capital of Slovene lands, encouraged a limited number of national publications in Slovene, particularly propaganda against Napoleon and the French. The first Slovene language newspaper was launched in 1797, followed by the publication of a Slovene dictionary in 1809. During that time Slovenes were also "in the process of articulating some kind of national awareness or autonomous cultural identity" that emphasized what Lonnie R. Johnson refers to as the "politics of language."[3]

The year 1809 saw most Slovene lands fall to Napoleon. The French tried to enforce the use of Croatian, but Slovene opposition caused the French to recognize the rights of Slovene language in administration and education. This clearly illustrates the growth and strength of Slovene ethnicity. A conspicuous Slovene national movement existed by the 1830s but struggled to enlist the growing middle class, and many arguments centered around the use of language.

By 1848, the idea of a United Slovenia emerged, which would be a separate kingdom that was part of the Habsburg Empire and would combine all ethnically Slovene territories. It is important to remember that those who create national boundaries do so with little regard to ethnicity, often with poor results. The movement also encouraged a separate diet for these lands and Slovene as the language of government and education. However, the movement lacked the larger central framework that the Croats and Serbs had and ultimately languished as a result. In the early 1850s, the absolutist regime "totally silenced the liberal minority, and proscribed the ideal of a United Slovenia as subversive of the established order of the traditional crownlands [*sic*]."[4]

In the 1860s, Slovenes gained "genuine strength from the widespread awakening of national consciousness among both peasants and townsmen," but the movement still lacked true political organization. Nevertheless, Slovenes representation increased in the national government, and by the late 1860s the United Slovenia movement was revived with large outdoor meetings in support. Again, though, rifts and clashes emerged that hurt the movement, this time between "Old Slovenes" and "Young Slovenes." There was no centralized, well-organized movement, yet there was clearly an ethnic identity that continued to grow and intensify throughout the remainder of the nineteenth century. The overarching theme of the movement was language use and rights and extending Slovene language to law, administration, religion, and education. Slovene literature and social criticism emerged during this period and became widely recognized and acknowledged.[5]

Slovene nationalism continued at the dawn of the twentieth century, but an unstable political atmosphere ruled throughout much of Europe, and Slovene territory shrank in size. "Although all Slovene political parties had before World War I endorsed the idea of association with other South Slavs, in almost all cases they had envisioned such a grouping within the Hungarian Empire."[6] The outcome of World War I rendered that argument void. Slovenes suffered greatly during that war, especially during the Battles of the Isonzo (1915–17) that occurred along the western border of Slovene lands. Over thirty thousand died in the fighting.

By the spring of 1917, a self-determination movement picked up steam, and a Slovene People's Party emerged. They demanded a somewhat independent state, but again, a lack of unity and a central organized movement and platform plagued real progress. However, on October 29, 1918, a declaration of an independent state of Slovenes, Croats, and Serbs was issued, and on October 31 a Slovene National Council replaced Austrian authority with a national government for the Slovene lands. It received no international recognition, and on December 1, 1918, they merged with Serbia and in 1929 took the name Yugoslavia. Slovenia remained part of Yugoslavia when it fell to communism in 1945. The "fall of Yugoslavia was complex and tragic" and had lasting consequences on the region.[7]

The fall of communism in 1989 had a monumental impact on the world. Since then, Poland, the Czech Republic, and Hungary have been regarded as the "big regional winners of the former Eastern bloc, but Slovenia should receive as much attention." In 1993, the Gross Domestic Product (GDP) of Slovenia was $6,490, while Croatia's was $1,900.[8] Slovenia became independent from Yugoslavia on June 25, 1991, and the European Union recognized its independence in 1992, the same year it was accepted as a member of the United Nations.[9]

Slovene Clergy and Their Impact on the Upper Great Lakes

Every ethnic group that encounters the American environment has its own impact on the people and the nation, and the Slovenes were no exception. Slovenes arrived in British America before the American Revolution, and their surnames appeared on General George Washington's payroll rosters during the American Revolution.

One of the major driving forces of the Slovene story in the nineteenth century was the role that the clergy played in the development of Catholicism in the Upper Great Lakes. The number of Slovene clergy stayed small until a migration of Catholic priests traveled to the Great Lakes and began to proselytize to American Indians. A number of Catholic missionaries visited the Upper Peninsula prior to the nineteenth century. The Jesuits arrived in the seventeenth century and maintained a presence in the Upper Peninsula, with varying degrees of saturation. These early missionaries paved the way for future Catholic missionaries such as Frederic Baraga. By the nineteenth century the Ojibwa knew who the Black Robes were and called upon them from time to time. The famous Slovene missionary called Michigan home from 1831 until his death in 1868. His activities are legendary among white Catholics, although many Native Americans have slightly different views. Along the way he established missions and claimed to baptize and convert thousands, even though he was not always welcome.

The Life of Frederic Baraga

Frederic Baraga was born on July 29, 1797. His family was moderately wealthy, and as the only son Baraga was heir to the family fortune and property. He started his early education at home under the guidance of his parents, particularly his pious mother.[10] He went to Ljubljana at the age of nine to study with a private tutor. Sadly he lost both parents a short time later—his mother when he was eleven and his father at fifteen.[11]

Baraga attracted the attention of Dr. George Dolinar, a professor of canon law. He took Baraga into his home. Upon turning nineteen, Baraga enrolled at the University of Vienna to study law. He also learned English, Italian, and Spanish. In addition to keeping his mind healthy, he committed himself to a rigorous physical routine and took almost daily long walks. His language and physical training helped him in his future missionary endeavors. Baraga also kept his appearance neat, shunned alcohol, and relaxed by painting.[12]

Both his education and the influence of his mother paved the way for Baraga's religious vocation, which was not his first career choice. He witnessed his mother's piety, kindness, charity, and devotion to God prior to her death.[13] Furthermore, while at the University of Vienna, he met the Redemptorist Blessed Clement Mary Hofbauer, who became Baraga's spiritual advisor. The Redemptorists aspired to live a simple Christian life and to spread the gospel to the poorest and most neglected souls in the world. Hofbauer greatly impacted Baraga.[14]

Baraga courted George Dolinar's daughter and asked for her hand in marriage. She agreed to marry him, and their engagement commenced. However, his final year of law school, the year leading up to the wedding, was one of great change in Baraga's life. He received the call to religious life. His decision was not hasty, and he took the time to ponder, consider, and pray about his decision. His choice to break off the engagement after he finished law school and enter seminary surprised many of his friends and relatives, and certainly his fiancée.[15] In 1821 he entered seminary. He gave away his inheritance to one of his sisters and refused to accept the small annuity she urged him to take. Baraga finished the three-year seminary program in two years and was ordained to the priesthood on September 21, 1823.[16]

Frederic Baraga Travels to America

Catholic priests, of course, cannot act on a whim, and Baraga could not simply leave Slovenia. He needed permission from two individuals—his own bishop and the bishop of the diocese he wished to enter, in this case Cincinnati. On August 10, 1829, he wrote to the bishop ordinariate in Ljubljana for permission to leave Slovenia in order to serve as a missionary to the Native Americans of the United States. Unconcerned about money or material goods, he left his homeland and arrived in New York City on New Year's Eve 1830 and made his way to Cincinnati, where his first task was to improve his English. In addition, a native speaker of Odawa tutored him. Eventually Baraga could speak Slovene, German, Latin, French, English, Italian, and seven separate Native American languages, and he and mastered the Ojibwa language to the point that he compiled a dictionary.[17] Near the end of May, 1831, he left Ohio for Michigan, and encountered Native American tribes for the first time. He wrote to his sister, "Happy day that placed me among the Indians, with whom I will now remain uninterruptedly to the last breath of my life."[18] So began thirty-seven years of missionary labors.

Baraga established his first mission at Harbor Springs, revitalizing a station that was originally established by Jesuits. Once the church was built, the next job was to set up a school. Acquiring and keeping teachers was not easy.[19] Baraga and other priests placed a high premium on education as a means of civilizing Native Americans. They also worked at settling Native Americans in stable communities. All missionaries found their work hindered by wandering Native Americans, many of whom, like the Ojibwa, followed seasonal cycles and moved when appropriate. Missionaries liked to teach Native Americans how to farm as well, which was difficult in the Northern Michigan climate and short growing seasons. Once basic needs were met, Baraga worked at getting blacksmiths and carpenters to the missions. He felt that the Ojibwa were adept at using their hands and in mechanical skills, and he sought to exploit that. The federal government later joined forces with missionaries, including Baraga, in providing blacksmiths and carpenters.[20] The mission at Harbor Springs grew while Baraga was in residence. According to the New Catholic Encyclopedia, "Baraga transformed the deteriorating mission of Harbor Springs into a model community."[21]

Missionaries faced severe trials in their work. Baraga was no exception, especially with the harsh winters in Northern Michigan. He often traveled

Photograph from 1867 of Bishop Baraga, with the effects of his stroke visible in his face. Credit: Central Upper Peninsula and Northern Michigan University Archives, Marquette, MI.

alone in the wilderness. Lodging was scarce, so he often slept outside. After he pulled his coat over his head and lay down in the snow, he sometimes woke up covered with several inches. Food was a problem as well, but it appears that Baraga had little appetite and generally ate bread and fish—never meat—and drank water.[22]

Baraga's next mission was established at Grand River, near the modern site of Grand Rapids. Things did not go well for Baraga at Grand River. He spent one of the most frightening nights of his life there as intoxicated Native Americans, at the urging of fur traders, tried to break into Baraga's cabin. He lamented in a letter to the Leopoldine Foundation the fact that fur traders kept the Native Americans at Grand River intoxicated with an unlimited supply of alcohol.[23] Baraga pleaded with the traders to stop doing so, and they threatened his life. He had a difficult time but claimed to make progress.[24] He had encountered the negative role that alcohol played among Native Americans, which had been a problem since the Jesuit missionaries and fur traders entered the countries centuries before.

Antonia Baraga

Antonia Baraga was the youngest of the Baraga children.[25] She married a knight of the Holy Roman Empire, Sir Felix Von Hoeffern, on May 31, 1824. Her brother presided at the ceremony. The marriage ended just a few short years later upon Felix's death. There were no children.

Her brother Frederic regularly wrote to his sisters and narrated his missionary activities. The letters deeply impressed Antonia. She gave up her rather leisurely life, gathered up as much capital as she could, and traveled to America to join Frederic. However, when she arrived in America, she learned that her brother was back in Europe. Baraga was surprised when he discovered his sister waiting for him when he returned in 1837.

At Antonia's first mission stops she distributed some of the wealth she had brought with her. Some of it was used to construct chapels. At Mackinac she established an industrial school where she taught Native American women how to sew, wash, bake, and cook. In addition, she apparently gained the trust and respect of many Native Americans. According to Msgr. F. A. O'Brien, if Native Americans traveled to Mackinac to talk to Frederic Baraga and he was absent, they went to Antonia. She left Mackinac and joined her brother at La Pointe, where smallpox broke out, infecting hundreds of Native Americans. Antonia labored incessantly for the ill, and her work has been credited to an increasing number of conversions.[26] However, she also contracted the disease, and that, coupled with the climate of Lake Superior, suggested to her doctors that perhaps a return to Europe was in order. She followed their advice.[27]

In the January 2, 1836, letter to Bishop Frederick Rese, Baraga lamented about issues that plagued both his and most other missionary's work—a lack of both money and personnel. He regretted the fact that he was alone in La Pointe, and although a school would benefit the mission greatly, he lacked a teacher. He stated, "A school would be very useful in this mission; but it is impossible for me to do both, to keep school and to perform properly my frequent mission duties and the visits to the sick."[28]

Baraga departed North America for Europe in 1837. Part of his mission was to gather donations of money and priests for his missionary endeavors. Catholic missionaries in the United States had to work much harder than many Protestant missionaries at generating money because they received little to no government aid for their work. Furthermore, while Catholic missionary societies were fewer in number than those for Protestants, what little money existed for Catholic missionary efforts was spread thin. Baraga also took advantage of his time in Europe to have a prayer book and a life of Christ that he wrote in Ojibwa published.[29] Baraga's writing, however, raised questions. He presented his work to a veteran missionary to the Algonquin Indians. The missionary found "serious mistakes in the expressions referring to the Holy Eucharist." Baraga agreed to correct the books prior to their distribution. The mistakes bothered Baraga to the point that he requested Bishop Rese to recall and destroy earlier copies of the books that Baraga had passed out while still in America.[30]

Baraga also worked among the Native Americans at La Pointe, in present-day Wisconsin. While there, some Native Americans entrusted him to prepare letters on their behalf. A principal chief of the area Ojibwa asked Baraga to write for him because "he has the confidence in me that I write them the most faithfully, and because he can understand me best of all when I translate to him in Indian the letters he receives and which are written in English or French.—So much for his copper-red majesty."[31] In the same letter he mentions the departure of his sister Antonia.[32]

Baraga's financial troubles continued at La Pointe. His European trip had been successful in terms of money raised for the missions. However, much of that money was pledged. There are several examples of money that never reached Baraga. The cardinal of Vienna caught on to the monetary issues as well. Instead of following the dictated way of sending money to missionaries through their bishop, he sent his donations to Baraga via the American Fur Company.[33]

The cardinal's decision to transfer money through the American Fur Company illustrates the extent to which many missionaries relied on outside secular help. This was especially true for Baraga for two reasons: the frontier location of his work and the fact that what little financial help he received was an ocean away. The American Fur Company and Baraga had an interesting relationship. Baraga deplored alcohol and its effects on Native Americans, and generally blamed fur traders for it. However, he behaved and acted prudently towards the American Fur Company because he knew his survival and the survival of his missions depended on them. Later Slovene immigrants, such as the Ruppe and Wertin families, would follow his example.

Ramsay Crooks was president of the American Fur Company from 1834 to 1859. He and Baraga were regular correspondents. Crooks did not mind helping missionaries out, as long as they did not "meddle with the trade."[34] Baraga called upon Crooks on numerous occasions for a variety of reasons. For example, when Baraga traveled to Europe in 1837, he took a book with him, now known as *Frederic Baraga's Short History of the North American Indians*. He had asked Crooks to secure some books to aid him in writing it, including Colden's *History of the Five Nations* and Heckwelder's narrative of his missionary activities.[35] Baraga always assured Crooks that he would pay for any and all services provided.

When Baraga returned from his European trip, he had a new source of potential income. It is ironic, considering Baraga's disdain of ardent spirits, that he funded his missions partly through wine and champagne sales. A Frenchman named Loisson donated twelve hundred bottles of wine and champagne to Baraga and sent them to America via the American Fur Company.[36] In a letter of May 5, 1838, Crooks informed Baraga that the wine had arrived. However, economic times were not at their best for wine and champagne sales, especially at ten dollars a bottle, and Crooks told Baraga that sales were quite low.[37] By 1840 sales still were not as Baraga hoped. Earlier he suggested that Crooks send the bulk of the wine west to see if it would sell better there. By late 1840 the suggestion turned to an order: "In some of my former letters I *advised* you, to send part of my wine to some places in the West. But in the present, I send you herewith an *express order* to send the whole of my Champagne—wine, on my risk, to the following places: Mackinac, Greenbay [*sic*], Milwaukee, Chicago, and Prairie de Chien."[38] The wine sold somewhat better after the price was dropped from ten dollars to seven dollars per bottle in 1843.[39] In 1844 the wine finally sold out. It appears as though the wine scheme never panned out as Baraga had hoped and never turned into a reliable source of money.

Baraga's relationship with the American Fur Company and Ramsay Crooks was productive and genial. Crooks appreciated the mutual benefits that the partnership between missionaries like Baraga and the American Fur Company provided. Obviously there were some self-serving benefits as well.

Fur traders often hoped missionaries could make their jobs easier by negotiating with or for the Native Americans on their behalf. That plan did not always work, because the men in the field and the president of the company were of entirely different character.

Indian Removal in the Upper Peninsula

Indian removal came late to the Upper Peninsula. The Indian Removal Act went into effect in 1830. However, it did not concern the Lake Superior Ojibwa right away. No resources of note were located in their lands, so there was no need to move them. However, that all changed when massive copper deposits were discovered in 1844. Missionaries had varying points of view about removal. Baraga generally thought it was a good idea, but only if there was a guarantee of continuous religious instruction. In 1848 the government wanted to move the Native Americans out of L'Anse. Baraga struggled mightily for five years to keep the mission where it was. He did not want to see his hard work vanish. To combat removal, Baraga decided to purchase the land his mission sat on. He called upon his friend Peter Barbeau for assistance. He wrote to Barbeau that he wished to purchase a "fraction of land lying in fractional Section No. 10 of Township No. 51, Range No. 33 West." The plot in question lay between land he had previously purchased from an independent landowner, and Baraga's own. He wanted the whole to be used for the benefit of his mission. He asked Barbeau to go to the Land Office to see exactly how much land there was and to secure it for him.[40]

The land issue was on the Native Americans minds as well. The Catholic Native Americans of L'Anse wrote to William Richmond, superintendent of Indian Affairs in Detroit: "We the Indians of the western side of Anse-Bay [*sic*] wish to know whether the lands around this Bay are to be sold this summer or not. Our missionary, the Rev. Frederic Baraga intends to buy for us a quarter of Section which we actually occupy, inhabit, and cultivate, and which he holds for us under the privilege of pre-emption right."[41]

The hardships associated with missionary work started catching up with Baraga by the end of the 1840s. His hearing was in decline, and he first mentioned deafness in 1853. Other ills also plagued him. He wrote to Bishop Peter Paul Lefevere in late 1848 to request a dispensation from fasting. In reply to the bishop's dispensation, Baraga wrote, "Formerly I could fast without much difficulty, even more rigorously than the Church prescribes."

He claimed to be up for the day no later than three o'clock in the morning. He spent the early hours in prayer and by writing. He felt obligated to provide Native Americans with ample reading material about religion once they learned to read. In early 1849 he put the finishing touches on a six-hundred-page book of "meditations on the virtues and on the good works of a Christian; on all the different sins, and on all the truths of our religion." He was pleased that he could write in "Indian" almost as well as in French. He also spent time on his Ojibwa dictionary, which he composed in Ojibwa, French, and English.[42]

Frederic Baraga Is Elevated to Bishop

By the 1850s, enough Catholics lived in the Upper Peninsula for the Vatican to consider creating a new diocese. Copper fever brought thousands of immigrants to the region. Baraga's name and reputation moved him to the top of the list of those considered for the position of bishop. In May 1852, the First Council of Baltimore petitioned Pope Pius IX to create a diocese and appoint a bishop in the Upper Peninsula.[43] The pope agreed, and Baraga was named first bishop of the new Diocese of Sault Sainte Marie and Marquette. Baraga's diary entries reveal a man none too thrilled with the appointment. However, he felt obligated to accept the position, although he was concerned about his missionary work carrying on as well.[44]

Baraga's first concern was the "spiritual misery of the Upper Peninsula" and the great shortage of priests. He traveled to Europe in late 1853 on a recruitment mission. He issued a report on the Lake Superior Missions to the *Detroit Catholic Vindicator* prior to his departure in which he provided an overview of his work, now spanning twenty-two years. His goal always was to start missions, get them off the ground and sustaining themselves, and then finally leave them in the capable hands of another missionary while he ventured off to new grounds. This report shows that he achieved those goals. At La Pointe he "brought into the sheep-fold of the Good Shepherd, by conversion and baptism, over seven hundred souls." In 1853 the mission survived under Father Skolla. He converted over three hundred at L'Anse and left it to Father Angelus Van Paemel, a man fluent in Ojibwa.[45]

Frederic Baraga felt that 1845 was a turning point in both the culture of the Upper Peninsula and in mission work. Until that time, he had spent his days teaching and preaching for Native Americans. However, in 1845 waves of immigrants moved to the Upper Peninsula to work in the copper mines. Many were Catholic, and Baraga could not tolerate "how destitute they were of the comforts and benefits of our holy religion." From that point on, he spent a great deal of time preaching at mining locations, although he never neglected Native Americans. The extra labor only punctuated the point that there was a great shortage of priests in the Upper Peninsula.[46]

He appealed to the Paris-based Society for the Propagation of the Faith for assistance during his European trip. He told them that he needed everything imaginable for a successful diocese: "churches, dwellings for the priests and school teachers, school houses, houses for brothers and sisters of different charitable activities, etc." Baraga prudently did not ask the society to pay for building construction—he stated that he could get the local population to do so at their expense. His main concern was his own cathedral. He admitted that it was a modest building that measured eighty feet by forty feet by twenty feet, located at the first see of the diocese in Sault Sainte Marie. In addition, he requested that the society defray the transportation for future priests of the diocese. Baraga hoped to find at least ten priests, but he was picky. Since English, French, German, and Ojibwa were spoken in the region, the priests had to speak at least some of those languages. Finally, he requested assistance with furniture, both for himself and the new priests. None of his requests seem unreasonable considering the fact that his was truly a frontier diocese.[47]

As bishop, Baraga maintained missionary work. He did not shy away from duty even in the face of the harshest conditions. In the winter he traveled by sleigh and on foot. In April 1855 he was called to the sick bed of a Native American on Bois-Blanc Island, three miles off shore from Mackinac. He traveled across the ice on horseback. In addition, he was often preoccupied with the state of education. Missionaries consistently sent him reports on the state of the schools at their missions, and the school at Sault Sainte Marie boasted 103 Native American students in 1855.[48]

With the exception of Baraga's elevation from a bishop of an apostolic vicariate to a bishop of a full-fledged diocese, the remainder of the 1850s was basically uneventful. Baraga spent his days taking care of both the diocese and the missions. In 1856 he performed the sacrament of confirmation for the first time with Native Americans. Prior to this there was little to no mention of that sacrament in his writings.[49]

Bishop Frederic Baraga lies in state in the original St. Peter Cathedral in Marquette, after his death on January 19, 1868. Credit: Antoine I. Rezek, History of the Diocese of Sault Ste. Marie and Marquette (Chicago: M.A. Donohue and Co., 1906).

By 1859 and 1860 Baraga's health started to falter. In a letter to the the Leopoldine Foundation, he discussed the speed with which stiffness and other ailments settled in, especially compared to his early years in the United States.[50] He still found solace in missionary work. In a letter to the Society for the Propagation of the Faith, he said, "I was obliged to perform the functions of a simple missionary at several mission stations. The bishop was completely forgotten." He enjoyed instructing catechumens, listening to confessions, baptizing, and celebrating mass.[51] He continued missionary work as the 1860s progressed and his health declined further. In 1862 he felt obligated to visit a mission himself "because the priest who is with me at the Saut [*sic*] does not speak Indian."[52] In addition, former mission stations called upon him to visit. In September 1865 Native Americans from the L'Anse mission sent him a letter that implored him to visit. They stated, "We think some time your [*sic*] have forgot us. And don't fail to come. We have a few words to address you and we know you shall give us a blessing and satisfaction."[53] Baraga discovered that the pope agreed to his request to move the see of his diocese from Sault Sainte Marie to Marquette at the end of 1865. He requested the transfer because of the increasing population in areas far west of Sault Sainte Marie and because Marquette was centrally located in the Upper Peninsula.[54]

Frederic Baraga's first official act of 1866 was to revise his will. He wanted Caspar Schulte, his assistant and a Native American, to take care of his possessions until his successor arrived, but he did not entrust him to execute his last will and testament. Baraga named two priests as executors.[55] Later that year, as he prepared for a council in Baltimore, he suffered a stroke. He felt obligated to go and endured the trip. He suffered another stroke in Baltimore and fell down a flight of stairs. As he fell his pectoral cross pierced his chest. He returned to Michigan even though he was urged to stay in Baltimore.[56] He spent the remainder of 1867 in great pain. He could no longer write for himself.[57] His hearing was nearly gone, and his head, hands, and feet were in constant pain.[58] As 1867 passed into 1868, Baraga and those around him knew the end was near. He only stood with assistance and switched between his bed and his chair in a futile search for comfort. His breathing was shallow and labored, and by January 9 he stopped eating. On January 19, 1868, Frederic Baraga passed away in Marquette.[59] His impact on the Upper Peninsula in total, and on Slovenes in particular, cannot be underestimated. His passing left a huge void for the people of the Diocese of Sault Ste. Marie and Marquette, but there was another Slovene waiting in the wings to take up Baraga's position.

Bishop Ignatius Mrak

Baraga's successor as bishop of the Diocese of Sault Ste. Marie and Marquette was also a Slovene, which made him one of the few non-Irish bishops in the United States at that time.[60] Ignatius Mrak was born in Carniola on October 16, 1808. His parents decided to have him pursue an education, and in 1825 he started to learn Latin. However, it appears that the seven-year-old struggled with the language, and his educational pursuits nearly ended before they began. Mrak preserved, and he successfully completed his course of study. In 1834 he enrolled in the seminary in Laibach. He graduated with honors in 1837 and was ordained to the priesthood on August 13 of that year. His Bishop, Anton Aloys Wolf, ordered him to celebrate his first mass in the town of Poelland, with "all secular pomp and worldliness be avoided."[61] As later events illustrate, this first example of modestly had a lasting effect on the young priest.

Before he took up a post as a parish priest, Mrak served for nearly two years as a tutor for the son of a baron. He returned to his priestly duties on January 27, 1840, and remained in that post until 1845. At that point, he had read about Baraga's work in North America and was inspired by it. He traveled to the United States in 1845 aboard the *Hindoo* and, after an eighty-five-day journey, arrived in New York on October 1. Then he traveled to Detroit and commenced his work in Michigan.

Father Mrak's first position in Michigan was as an assistant to his countryman Father Pierz in Arbre Croche. Mrak was eager to learn a Native American language, and apparently his childhood language struggles abandoned him. In a report to the Leopoldine Foundation, Pierz remarked that after ten days of study, Mrak delivered a sermon in the language he had just started to study, using notes provided by Pierz. As his proficiency progressed, the decision was made to make better use of Mrak's talents. The number of Indian converts increased, but they were spread over a wide area. Therefore, Pierz and Mrak, with the blessings of Bishop Lefevere, divided their mission into two separate areas, so they could make better use of their time, talent, and resources. By 1851, Pierz had left Michigan to go to Minnesota, but Mrak remained as a missionary.

Frederic Baraga knew his fellow Slovene and was impressed by him. On November 20, 1859, Baraga promoted Mrak to the post of vicar general. One Mrak's first duties in his new assignment was a trip home to Slovenia both to visit his family and, more importantly, to try to recruit new missionaries for the diocese. Baraga ordered him, "that he may above all other things, seek missionaries, of whom there is a great scarcity."[62] This was a perennial problem that plagued missionary activities in the Great Lakes throughout the nineteenth century.

For reasons lost to the historical record, Mrak became disenchanted with missionary life, and in 1863 he wrote to Baraga to inform him that he planned on leaving not only his Indian mission but also the United States as soon as the weather allowed. Obviously this news distressed Baraga greatly, and he endeavored to change Mrak's mind. Baraga also wrote to Bishop Lefevere to ask for his intervention. He stated, in part, that he told Mrak "that he could not leave now our missions with good conscience, as he knows well all the languages that are necessary there. I request your Lordship to recommend him earnestly to remain in our missions. I also beg your Lordship to ask him the true reason of so strange an intention of going back to his own country."[63] The "true reason" was never revealed, but Mrak indeed did change his mind and remained in the mission.

When Frederic Baraga died in 1868, a new leader for the Diocese of Sault Ste. Marie and Marquette was needed. By all accounts and evidence, Mrak proved a reluctant choice, although he was qualified and appointed by the pope. A number of letters to Mrak that announced his appointment went unanswered, and more than one bishop reached out to him to answer the call. One letter reminded Mrak that, "All are anxious that you should accept—and the Holy Father will be distressed and displeased if you refuse." After Christmas of 1868, Mrak finally resigned himself to his fate and left for Cincinnati to be installed as bishop. He arrived in February and was elevated on February 7, 1869.

Bishop Mrak first appeared in his new role in March when he arrived in Escanaba. According to the account, his humble and modest style caused a rather embarrassing moment. He entered a house next to the cathedral dressed in a "fur cap drawn over his ears, a shabby ulster, a colored shawl around his neck and a pair of lumbermen's mitts, all of questionable antiquity."[64] A woman who was present and in charge of cooking the meal did not believe that Mrak was the bishop, and it took two other priests to convince her of the truth. The new bishop waited a week after his arrival in Marquette before holding his first mass as bishop in his new diocese, due to a delay in the arrival of many of his possessions from his trip to Cincinnati. On March 7 he celebrated his inaugural mass.

The data that Rezek provides shows that Mrak inherited a diocese with fourteen priests scattered between eighteen churches, with a Catholic population of twenty thousand. The shortage of priests scattered across such a vast wilderness caused the new bishop no small amount of consternation. That being said, he was no fool, and he was as stubborn and picky as his predecessor had been, regardless of the circumstances. He demanded excellence and expected the highest levels of competence from his priests. This is illustrated in an episode that took place not long after he became bishop. Even though technically in the Lower Peninsula of Michigan, Beaver Island in Lake Michigan was originally under Mrak's domain. At that time, he discovered that three priests in his diocese had been ordained with less than the regular amount of required theological training. He called two of them in for an examination. They failed miserably and were subsequently dismissed. The third was a popular Irish priest on Beaver Island. The parishioners were worried about losing him and did not care about his lack of proper training. They schemed when they learned that Mrak was visiting the island personally to examine the priest and convinced him that the ferryboat might not be able to take him back to the mainland for a month if he traveled to the island. Mrak realized the hostility of the situation and decided to not travel to Beaver Island. However, upon his return to Marquette, he passed both the Irish priest and Beaver Island out of his jurisdiction. He kept quite the careful eye on whom he allowed to be ordained, and his efforts proved to be successful. The second priest he ordained was a Slovene named John N. Stariha, who was eventually elevated to the position of bishop in South Dakota.[65]

The year 1869 continued to be incredibly busy for the new Slovene bishop. He was called to Rome to participate in a council held at the Vatican. He left Father Edward Jacker in charge while he was away, and in September he left for Rome. On his return trip, he visited Slovenia and obtained a student for the priesthood, Luke Mozina. The boat that they traveled on stopped in

Bishop Ignatius Mrak near the end of his life. Credit: Antoine I. Rezek, History of the Diocese of Sault Ste. Marie and Marquette (Chicago: M.A. Donohue and Co., 1906).

Sicily, and Mrak presented himself to the local priest. He was informed that no bishop had visited there in many years, and to celebrate the occasion, the townspeople held a parade. At the same time, the fellow Catholics in his diocese grew more and more worried. Mrak's absence was long, and he did not write back to Michigan while he was in Europe. As such, Jacker feared and prepared for the worst. He arranged to have someone else ordained bishop in Green Bay. He sent the future bishop Frederick Eis with a letter that explained the circumstances to Green Bay, but Mrak arrived back in Marquette in October, to the relief of many.

Upon Mrak's return, he found that the poor state of diocesan finances had to be dealt with. This was an issue that Baraga had faced and that Mrak's successors faced as well. At one point, the pastor responsible for the parishes in Negaunee and Ishpeming was ordered to remain in his post for five years, during which time he would be responsible for the existing debt of both churches. To help offset the debt, Mrak suggested soliciting gifts from parishioners, and the idea of renting pews was floated. Regardless of the order from the bishop, the priest left the diocese the following year and left behind a debt of some fifteen thousand dollars. Mrak then appointed Rev. John Vertin, a Slovene who would ultimately succeed him as the third bishop of the diocese to fill the vacancy.

Mrak's frugal ways and modesty influenced all parts of his episcopacy. Like Baraga before him, he was quite strict with his priests and expected them not only to obey church doctrine but to be model Catholics for their parishioners. He felt that "any tendency on the part of his priests to accumulate money was . . . a fault, for he believed . . . that godliness with contentment is great gain."[66] To further the cause of improving diocesan finances, he issued a circular in 1875 that called for quite specific ways for parishes to be run and for elections for councilors to oversee many church functions, including assisting with financial solvency. In addition, he called for his personal authorization for certain expenses, including monetary layouts over one hundred dollars that were not in the original budget, and building or enlarging a church.

No matter how hard he tried, the financial situation of the Diocese of Sault Ste. Marie and Marquette did not improve during his reign as bishop. A number of schools closed due to these hardships, although Mrak valiantly tried to reopen at least two of them. Some of the closed schools had actually been somewhat prosperous, but a nationwide depression in the 1870s hit the Upper Peninsula as well and caused further struggles for the bishop. Schools were closed in both Sault Ste. Marie and in Hancock. At the same time, the number of missions in the diocese increased, but there were not enough priests to proselytize to the people. Even with these difficulties, Mrak maintained high standards as well as a tight grip on the operations of his diocese. For example, a church in Hancock had some peculiar interactions between the priest and the laity. According to Rezek,

> Bishop Mrak met this spirit of insubordination promptly, calling upon the deluded members of the congregation at once to submit to the ecclesiastical authority, and when they failed to obey, he placed the church under interdict and pronounced canonical penalties upon the ringleaders and all those who resisted his authority.[67]

Recalling that Mrak seemed loathe to accept the position of bishop in the first place, it is little wonder such events taxed the man and his mind, as well as his resolve. He longed for his previous role as a missionary. In addition, he was approaching the age of sixty-five, although by all accounts he was a strong and energetic man. After nearly a decade of serving as bishop, he decided to resign. His health finally started to fail a bit, and during the winter of 1877–78, he suffered an attack of sciatic rheumatism that incapacitated him for nearly six months. He resigned in 1879, and Rev. Edward Jacker was named the temporary administrator of the diocese. Fellow Slovene Rev. John Vertin was appointed the third bishop of the Diocese of Sault Ste. Marie and Marquette.

In his retirement, Mrak's religious fervor and devotion never faltered. He started retirement by serving as priest in Negaunee, because Bishop Vertin implored him to stay around due to the extreme shortage of priests. He remained there until September 1880, when he temporarily took over the church in Menominee. Afterward, he lived with Vertin until 1883. During that time, his health improved, and he moved to the Diocese of Grand Rapids to serve, as he had originally done in Michigan, as a missionary to the Indians. He served in that capacity for many years, until he returned to Marquette on September 1, 1891, to administer his old diocese while Bishop Vertin was in Rome. He lived in St. Mary's Hospital in Marquette, and served as a chaplain while he was there. Finally, his health truly started to fail, and he passed away on January 2, 1901, at the age of eighty-nine. *The Daily Mining Journal* reported his death the following day, and reported that although he had been comatose for several weeks, he had full use of his faculties just before he passed.[68] Two days later, that newspaper reported his funeral services. They lamented that

> the older people recall the period of his active labors but the younger generations have grown away from him and they must gain an idea of the great humility and usefulness of his life from story and the relation of incident. There does not appear to be any satisfactory sketch of Bishop Mrak's life extant although his labors with the Indians and as a bishop of this diocese in its early days were second in importance only to those of the famous Bishop Baraga.[69]

A few weeks later, the *Weekly Mining Journal* reprinted a tribute to Mrak that had appeared in the *Michigan Catholic* published in Detroit. It stated that, "This grand old saint of the upper peninsula, now dead, was a man of so much humility that upon his demise the newspapers of his diocese that sought to honor him could not find satisfactory material for a sketch of his life. He had literally effaced himself."[70]

The Slovene priest, missionary, and bishop played a large role in the development of the Upper Peninsula, especially for the over twenty thousand Catholics that were counted during his episcopacy. However, his successor, Rev. John Vertin, and the Vertin family, were to have an arguably larger impact.

The Wertin Family and Bishop John Vertin

The future third Bishop of the Diocese of Sault Ste. Marie and Marquette, and the third consecutive Slovene to hold that post, was also born in Carniola, on July 17, 1844, to Joseph and Mary Vertin. He had three siblings: Joseph, Mary, and George. His siblings spelled their surname as Wertin. Rezek states that the discrepancy is due to the fact that the original spelling in Slovene is with a "V," but the bishop's siblings, unlike the bishop himself, chose to spell the name with the phonetic "W."[71]

Prior to their immigration to America, the Vertins were rich in land holdings, but their lands produced less and less as time progressed. The patriarch of the family, Joseph, sought to improve the family's fortunes and started a dry goods business. He traveled throughout Bavaria and Saxony and even ventured into Switzerland, where he sold goods from a backpack. Then, as a result of the opportunities provided by the Gold Rush in California, he traveled to America in 1852 and spent the next five years in the West. In 1857 he returned home, and found his son John engaged in education, and decided to provide him with the best education that he could.

Joseph decided to travel to America again to continue his business. Supposedly Frederic Baraga himself suggested that he try his luck in the Copper Country. Baraga encountered Vertin and Peter Ruppe, who both resided in Chicago and who both complained about the poor business prospects

Advertisement for the Vertin Brothers Department Store in Calumet. This image shows the building after two upper stories were added. Credit: Keweenaw Digital Archives, Michigan Technological University Archives and Copper Country Historical Collections, Houghton, MI.

in Chicago. Baraga suggested that they go to the Upper Peninsula, perhaps Marquette, where a new iron mine had opened. Both men purchased a great deal of merchandise in Chicago and traveled to Marquette. In 1858 Vertin moved to Houghton, invested in copper mines, and became quite wealthy, and then sent word to his family to join him.[72] On July 7, 1863, his wife and four children arrived in New York and departed for Houghton.

Ivan Molek, a Slovene immigrant who arrived in Calumet in 1903, also recounted another version of this story. Molek visited a saloonkeeper named Miha Klobuchar, a fellow Slovene, who told him that Bishop Baraga visited Chicago and met Vertin and Ruppe, who complained to him about the Civil War's effects on their business. Baraga told them all about the Copper Country and the mining explosion. Vertin and Ruppe took his advice. Klobuchar added details to the story that Rezek and others left out. For example, at that time, the train only went as far as Milwaukee, so both men had to take horses and wagons for the rest of their journey. They opened a store, and as Baraga had predicted, business was good.

John Vertin was about to begin philosophical studies when he left Slovenia for America. He wanted to study for the priesthood and found a willing sponsor in his countryman Bishop Frederic Baraga. He learned philosophy under the tutelage of Father Cebul, who was stationed in Wisconsin. In the summer of 1864, John asked to go to Negaunee to study with a priest who was fluent in French in order to perfect his own study of that language. That fall, Vertin returned to Wisconsin to officially begin studying for the priesthood, into which Bishop Baraga ordained him on August 31, 1866. He has the distinctions of being the first priest ordained in the city of Marquette and the last to be ordained by Baraga.

Father Vertin's first assignment was to Houghton. While he was there, he enlarged the church considerably in size. In 1871, Bishop Mrak called him to Negaunee, which, as stated previously, had incurred a debt of over fifteen thousand dollars.[73] Luckily, Vertin seemed to have inherited some of his father's business acumen, and by 1874, he lowered the debt to the point that he was able to construct a priest's home. Less than seven years after taking charge, the debt was less than two thousand dollars.

It is surely unique in the annals of United States Catholic History that the first three bishops of a diocese had the same international heritage, but that is precisely what the Diocese of Sault Ste. Marie and Marquette can boast. Once Bishop Mrak resigned, there was a new opening for the leader of Upper Michigan's Catholics. The third Slovene in a row, Rev. John Vertin, was chosen. He was raised to the episcopacy at the age of thirty-five, making him the youngest bishop in North America at that time, and he remains one of the youngest ever in the history of Roman Catholicism.[74]

Like his Slovene predecessor, Vertin was not excited about the prospect of running a diocese. Antoine Rezek, who personally knew Vertin and was in fact ordained by him, stated that he was "loathe to accept." In Vertin's own words, "I have not as yet made up my mind to accept the episcopal *onus* on my weak and unworthy shoulders and if I must tell you the truth, I am not at present more inclined to accept. The diverse difficulties of this poor diocese were always more or less perplexing, but they are now worse than ever."[75] Nevertheless, he resigned himself to his new position and was consecrated on September 14, 1879, in Negaunee. That was the first time such an event occurred in the Upper Peninsula, and the masses turned out.

Vertin planned to travel to Marquette on Sunday, October 5, 1879. However, on Thursday, October 2, the cathedral burned to the ground. According to the *Mining Journal*, the fire started sometime before four o'clock in

Bishop John Vertin at the time of his consecration, 1879. Credit: Antoine I. Rezek, History of the Diocese of Sault Ste. Marie and Marquette (Chicago: M.A. Donohue and Co., 1906).

the morning, and by the time people realized what was going on, it was too late to save the building. That was the church that Bishop Baraga himself had started prior to his death. Arson was ruled to be the cause of the blaze, yet no culprit was ever identified. Circumstantial evidence suggested that those who were angry at the order to move Father John C. Kenny—who had recently been removed from his position as pastor by Vertin—were at fault, but no firm proof ever solidified. A large portion of his congregation was obviously upset at his move, but Bishop Vertin refused to change his mind, and Kenny left.[76]

Bishop Vertin inherited a diocese in financial peril, and with a Catholic population that remained virtually unchanged since Mrak's episcopacy. Eighteen priests served twenty-eight churches. He oversaw a period of growth in the diocese, but had a great deal of work to do from the outset. He needed to attract priests, and he also demanded stable finances. To that end, he did not allow a priest to serve any location that could not afford to pay the priest's salary, which he fixed at eight hundred dollars. He also needed a new cathedral. He received permission from Rome to levy a tithing on each congregation to offset both the expenses of the diocese and the building of the new cathedral. Plans for the new church were printed in the *Mining Journal* on January 15, 1881. It was to be one hundred sixty feet by eighty feet, with two towers of 132½ feet in height, all covered by Marquette sandstone. In 1881, the cost of the building, sans any furniture or adornments, was estimated at $40,000.00.[77]

Tithing alone would not allow construction to begin. Bishop Vertin relied on donations from a variety of sources, including his father Joseph, and many of his and his family's personal friends, regardless of creed, sent what they could. He also issued a circular that proclaimed that anyone who donated at least fifty dollars would have their names written in a memorial book and have a mass said for their intention for a period of ten years. In addition to individual donations, all the parishes of the diocese submitted money from special collections, and a number of priests sent in personal donations as well. On Sunday, June 19, 1881, Vertin oversaw the cornerstone laying ceremony, which was attended by over five thousand people.[78] By the fall of 1883, the church was enclosed under a roof, and by Christmas of that year, the basement hosted services. In thanksgiving, the bishop printed a thank you message in the *Mining Journal* and noted those who had donated more than one hundred dollars, a list that included the likes of Peter White, Jacob Frei, and Martin Vierling.

In addition to overseeing a growing diocese and the construction of a new cathedral, Vertin had many other duties as a bishop. For example, right after the cornerstone ceremony of the new cathedral, he had to go to Rome for an official visit, which was his first visit to Europe since leaving Slovenia for America.[79] He also attended the Third Plenary Council of American Bishops in Baltimore, which was held in the fall of 1884. He served on a committee in charge of drawing up decrees about certain aspects of Christian doctrine. He then saw to it that the new doctrines and decrees were upheld in his own diocese. Of particular importance to him were those related to education. He stated that, "One of the chief duties are those of the parents towards their children, and of the children towards their parents." He issued a lengthy pastoral letter in 1884 that testified to this belief and admonished Catholics to begin educating their children from birth and that this education should last a lifetime. Vertin also understood the importance of a strong Catholic educational foundation, and whenever possible made sure that a school was opened. In those locations that could not afford a school, he instructed the priests to give "regular Catechetical instruction on Saturdays and Sundays."[80] In addition, he asked priests to hear children's confessions at certain times throughout the liturgical year. The bishop expected many things from his priests regarding education, and it certainly had a positive effect on the spiritual lives of the Catholics in the diocese.[81]

After being bishop of the Diocese of Sault Ste. Marie and Marquette for ten years, John Vertin found his diocese in much better shape than when he started and witnessed a great deal of growth. He decided to reevaluate the governance of the Catholic Church in the Upper Peninsula and held a conference at the still unfinished St. Peter's Cathedral to discuss a variety of issues. Some of these included taxes and fees, such as a minimum charge of five dollars for marriages with an additional five dollars charged for a Nuptial High Mass; an "Infirm Priest's Fund"; and a decree that all Catholic children must attend Catholic schools as soon as they have received their first communion.

The opening of the next decade of Vertin's episcopacy found the cathedral ready to be reopened. In the spring of 1890, the furnishings and adornments, including frescoes, were in place, and on the morning of Sunday, July 27, 1890, trains arrived from all over the diocese that brought the masses to the dedication mass. The following year, Vertin celebrated the twenty-fifth anniversary of his ordination to the priesthood. True to his character, he opposed any celebration, and stated, "if it were the 25th anniversary of my bishopric it might be worthy of special notice, but in the twenty five years as a priest I have done nothing to merit any extraordinary honors."[82] Regardless of his wishes, both priests and laypeople defied the bishop's orders and clandestinely planned a celebration that took place on September 1, 1891. The front page of the *Weekly Mining Journal* featured an in-depth story about the silver jubilee celebration. The *Weekly Mining Journal* also reminded its readers that Vertin used all of his private fortune to help build the new cathedral. In addition, they reported that the diocese at that time had fifty-six priests, fifty churches, sixty-five stations, one "young ladies academy," seventeen schools that served over four thousand students, two orphanages, and a Catholic population of sixty thousand.

The priests of the diocese pooled their resources together and purchased Vertin an outfit reported to have cost nearly twenty-five hundred dollars. The people of the Upper Peninsula, Catholic and non-Catholic, raised around four thousand five hundred dollars in part to offset the trip to Rome he had to take right after the celebration.[83] Before he could leave, however, he endured a celebration that saw St. Peter's Cathedral filled beyond capacity. His parents and brother were in attendance from the Copper Country and joined Marquette leaders such as Peter White and J. M. Longyear. All of those who attended the celebration left with a menu card that featured a likeness of the bishop, a biography of his life, and a vision of the new cathedral. Overall, it was a fitting tribute to a man whose episcopacy had achieved so much in such a relatively short time.

The historical record of Bishop Vertin thins somewhat during the eight years that transpired between his silver jubilee and his death in 1899 at the age of fifty-four. Part of the reason is that his health started to fail around the middle of that decade. He continued to write circulars for his priests and is said to have never "lost sight of the many sacrifices which the priest (those in his diocese) was expected to make daily for the sake of his flock."[84] He inherited large estates when his parents passed away, followed by the death of his brother in 1895. He sought out many treatments from many doctors and traveled to a number of "health-resorts," but to no avail. He passed away on Sunday, February 26, 1899, due to heart failure. Less than an hour after his death, news had spread throughout Marquette, and the cathedral was filled with mourners. A crowd estimated at over two thousand that filled St. Peter's Cathedral to "suffocation" attended his funeral, and many hundreds more filled the streets outside. The *Weekly Mining Journal* remarked,

> The crowd embraced not only the regular attendants at the cathedral, but those of other church affiliations and still more who have no church con-

> nections at all. It included people in all walks of life, and in many instances the man of wealth and the day laborer, each unable to find a seat, stood side by side during the long services, and together paid homage to the reverend dead.[85]

The mass lasted nearly three hours and was presided over by the Archbishop of Milwaukee, with five bishops, including Ignatius Mrak, in attendance.

Bishop Vertin oversaw a period of great growth for the Diocese of Sault Ste. Marie and Marquette. He ordained nine priests between 1880–90 and nearly thirty more in the final nine years of his life. He benefitted from a booming mining industry, to be sure, but he deserves credit for the adroit way he handled the internal workings of the Catholic Church. New mines opened throughout the Upper Peninsula, and he often visited places that requested new churches to determine the size required, as well as the sustainability of a parish in a given location. Most of those parishes were upstarts with little to no resources of their own. Again, the Vertin business acumen kicked in, and Vertin tended to be somewhat generous in sponsoring new parishes. According to Rezek, "he always went sponsor for any reasonable amount of debt, and as the property was deeded to him in fee simple he personally signed the notes and never mortgaged any property."[86] By the time his episcopacy ended, the value of property held by the diocese was over seven hundred thousand dollars, with less than fifty thousand dollars in debt. In addition to churches, he valued, encouraged, and supported parochial schools. These institutions were implemented in a number of locations, including Houghton, Ishpeming, Negaunee, and Escanaba.

The *Weekly Mining Journal* reminded its readers of his accomplishments when they reported his funeral services. Recalling the numbers that Bishop Vertin started his episcopacy with, it is quite impressive to consider that, in 1899, there were nearly seventy-five thousand white Catholics in the Diocese of Sault Ste. Marie and Marquette, around three thousand Native Americans who were practicing Catholics, and sixty priests serving fifty churches and over seventy other stations. "He has not only seen the growth of his beloved church keep pace with the educational and industrial advancement of the peninsula, but he has been largely instrumental in building it up, till the church in this section stands as the peer of the church in any other section of the country."[87] Two years later, upon the death of Ignatius Mrak, the *Daily*

Mining Journal reported on the continued growth of the diocese. Even after Vertin's death, the seeds that he helped plant and the resulting fruit continued to multiply. At that time, there were nearly seventy priests serving fifty-six churches and over five thousand five hundred students enrolled in Catholic schools.[88] The fourth bishop of the Diocese of Sault Ste. Marie and Marquette, Rev. Frederick Eis of Germany, inherited a much better situation thanks to the labors of John Vertin, his Slovene predecessor.

The Role of Slovene Clergy

These three Slovene clerics were important to the development of Catholicism in the Upper Great Lakes, but there were many other Slovene clergy who traveled to the United States upon the invitation of Baraga, Mrak, and Vertin. Their first task was ministering to the Catholics of the region. Given their backgrounds and education, these priests were fluent in Slovene and related Slavic tongues, in addition to German and French. This linguistic skill, perhaps exemplified best by Baraga, helped them learn English and Native American dialects. This was also important because of the multilingual backgrounds of the Catholic population in the mining regions of the Upper Peninsula. For example, Rev. Peter Sprajcar was pastor at Holy Family Church in Ironwood, and he ministered in Slovene, Slovak, Bohemian, and German.

The Slovene clergy, led by Baraga, also had a profound cultural impact on Michigan. Baraga developed a large library, and his intellectual abilities and writings led to the creation of a vast amount of materials related to the culture of Native Americans. In addition, the Franciscan missionary Rev. Skolla, who worked alongside Baraga upon his arrival in the United States in 1854, was a talented painter and poet. Rev. Antoine J. Rezek was a priest at the bustling St. Ignatius in Houghton and found time to research and write the monumental two-volume *History of the Diocese of Sault Ste. Marie and Marquette*, which remains the essential work on the history of the diocese.

Slovenes in the Upper Peninsula

The Slovenes who came to Michigan were involved primarily in four occupations: mining, manufacturing, lumber, and commerce. The Copper Country was home to thousands of Slovene immigrants who were originally attracted to the region by the information provided by Frederic Baraga, and by the economic boom that had set in with the opening of copper mines. Although most were employed as miners, a number of them became entrepreneurs and community leaders. Two of the most prominent early settlers were Peter Ruppe and Joseph Vertin, and throughout their lives, both families interacted greatly.

It is somewhat difficult to find good first-hand accounts of Slovene life in the Copper Country from the late nineteenth and into the early twentieth centuries. However, a few solid examples survived to the present day. One example comes from Ivan Molek. His wife Mary translated his autobiographical sketches and published them in 1979.[89] His story provides a fascinating glimpse into immigrant life in Calumet during the first decade of the twentieth century.

Ivan Molek

Ivan Molek was born in 1882 in Slovenia. He decided to leave Slovenia around his eighteenth birthday to improve his fortunes, like the majority of immigrants. He had never intended to remain permanently in the United States; rather, he had hoped to earn more money than he ever could in his homeland and return in a much better position. He was not the first of his family to make the trip across the Atlantic Ocean; a number of his family were already in the United States, but their fortunes had not fared so well. Many of them worked in mines, including some in the Copper Country. He left Slovenia in 1900 and started his life in the United States in a Pennsylvania factory. He remarked that even though his standard of living was quite low by American standards, it was much better than anything he experienced in Slovenia. The main issue was a lack of steady employment, and Molek wanted a better chance. Many of his family lived in Calumet, including an aunt, uncle, and cousins. He wrote to them and inquired about the work situation and the prospects of steady employment. In addition, he needed a loan to travel from Pennsylvania to Michigan. The return message included a promise of steady employment and a money order for the train.[90]

While traveling from Pennsylvania to Calumet, his train stopped in Chicago. A man stopped him and asked where he was going. Molek told him, and the man exclaimed, "Jesus Christ! It's winter there. It's always Siberia there." The man then took him into a shop and tried to properly outfit him for the Northern Michigan weather. However, Molek had only three dollars and could not afford the fifteen-dollar topcoat the man suggested.[91] Once back on the train, Molek was amazed at the vast distances between towns in the United States. It was so different for Molek to travel hundreds of miles and still be in the same country.

Ivan Molek arrived in Calumet on May 2, 1903. At that time the city was a booming center of copper mining. As soon as he disembarked the train, he saw a sign that read, "Mihael Schmalzel, Slovenian Tavern." As he walked toward his aunt and uncle's house, he passed the Vertin Brothers Department Store and described it as a "palace." An advertisement called it the largest department store north of Milwaukee, and Molek believed it. Before he arrived at his family's home, he also passed the remains of the Slovene church that had burned the previous year.

Running boarding houses and accommodating those needing a place to live was a common occupation for immigrants, including Molek's family. There were three boarders living in the house with them—all miners. He visited the Red Jacket Shaft, owned by Calumet & Hecla, the following morning. He was amazed to discover that it was not iron ore, as he had thought, but rather copper, that was the main product of the mining industry. Nevertheless, he arrived with his uncle fully expecting to go to work. However, he was told that he would have to wait "some weeks" to begin work.[92]

Rather than sullenly await better prospects, Molek decided to learn as much as he could about his new home. His recollections provide a wealth of information on the Copper Country. One account deserves to be quoted at length:

> I soon observed that "our company" and "our copper" expressed some kind of local patriotism in general, while, individually, the miners differentiated one another by the mind in which he worked. Whoever was employed by the mighty Calumet & Heclas [*sic*] had reached the highest rung on the ladder. Miners at a smaller and less wealthy company were on a lower social scale . . . There was something concrete about this discrimination. C. & H. [Calumet & Hecla] paid the highest wages and had the best equipment; consequently the work was also much easier.[93]

He also discovered that he lived in a thriving city of some 65,000 inhabitants, or so he estimated. The more accurate figure is around 25,000. Mining was the way of life, and ruled most people's existences. Some miners lived in company towns where their rent was taken from their paychecks. If they lost their jobs, they also lost their homes.

In his memoir, Molek provides an interesting history of Calumet. He claimed that it was the second oldest Slovene settlement in the United States, after Brockway, Minnesota. The first two Slovenes who arrived in the area were Ruppe and Vertin. By the time Molek arrived in Calumet, the businesses started by both men were still thriving, and Peter Ruppe's son, also named Peter, was a millionaire.[94]

Molek lived in Calumet for only two years. He stated that during that time the Slovene community there reached its zenith, and numbered around twelve thousand people. He counted forty Slovene businesses, including taverns, grocery and department stores, and butcher shops. There were

Peter Ruppe Jr.

Calumet civic leader Peter Ruppe Jr., who was the son of one of the original Slovene settlers in the area. Credit: Keweenaw Digital Archives, Michigan Technological University Archives and Copper Country Historical Collections, Houghton, MI.

Peter Ruppe Jr., whose father moved to Copper Country at Frederic Baraga's suggestion, was born in Slovenia in 1843. When he turned seventeen he left to join his father in America. He worked for his father and then tried his hand at mining. He earned sixty dollars per month at the Quincy mine and then moved on to the Delaware mine. He saved three hundred dollars and decided to move to Chicago to start a business and make his fortune. Things did not go well, and he returned to Michigan. He went to a business college and learned a great deal about the American business environment. Things got much more lucrative for him after that, and he started a store in Calumet on May 18, 1869.* Marie Prisland credits Ruppe with being the "First Slovenian Millionaire." She states that he invested in the Calumet Mining Company before it merged with the Hecla Mining Company. When that occurred, the stock that he had purchased for ten dollars a share was worth one thousand dollars a share. In 1900 a copper vein was discovered in Arizona, and he invested in that as well, at one dollar a share. He later sold thousands of shares at two hundred dollars each and became a millionaire.†

*Evening News Association, *Men of Progress: Embracing Biographical Sketches of Representative Michigan Men, with an Outline History of the State* (Detroit: Evening News Association, 1900), 182.

†Marie Prisland, *From Slovenia—to America* (Chicago: Slovenian Women's Union of America, 1968), 111–12.

Slovene benefit societies and a Slovene-language newspaper. Interestingly, the Calumet & Hecla Mining Company provided a Slovene library for their employees to use. Clearly, a strong Slovene ethnic presence was in place, and other Slovene immigrants attested to this as well.

As stated earlier, one of the difficulties in ferreting out the Slovene story in Michigan is the confusion in the records, since most Slovenes are listed as

Austrian. Molek illustrates this: He befriended one of the Vertin brothers and frequented their store, which was four stories tall and employed a number of Slovenes. However, other stores employed Slovenes as well and liked to boast that "Austrian" was spoken at their establishments.[95]

On one of his walks through Calumet, Molek discovered something that would have large implications on his life later. While in Pennsylvania, he had heard that a Slovene newspaper was published somewhere in Michigan. While walking down Seventh Street, he noticed a building with a sign that said, "Glasnik Publishing Company." He stopped by the saloon that he noticed upon his first arrival and inquired about it. He learned that Glasnik Publishing Company was a Slovene business that had been publishing a Slovene newspaper for the past three years. Molek had an interest in writing, and the editor of the Slovene paper told him that he was welcome to submit things for the weekly publication. He visited the office and met a man named Maks Buh, who was the nephew of another famous Slovene missionary, a contemporary of Frederic Baraga named Joseph Buh.

Molek Enters the Mine

Exactly one month after he first saw a mine, Ivan Molek was called to work in one. He went with a family member to the Vertin brothers store to buy what he needed, with money loaned to him from his family. He bought a coat, trousers, shirt, underwear, and a hat. He stated, "The hat was the most interesting item. It was of a stiff resinous cloth. Above the forehead was a piece of tinplate into which the lamp was stuck. Of course, a small tin lamp must be bought, too, fueled by some kind of grease."[96] He also purchased a pair of boots. On Monday morning he went to the Red Jacket Shaft. He was sent to Shaft No. 63 and ordered to load copper rocks into a bucket. His partner was not his kin but a countryman nonetheless.

The pressure changes as he descended down the mine caused Molek discomfort, but it abated. He discovered benches along the shafts, along with cross-ventilation tunnels that made the air somewhat fresh and cool, but that changed once he descended into Shaft No. 63. A five-minute walk bathed him in sweat, and the air was "hot and oppressive."[97] He arrived in his assigned spot and started shoveling rock into a bucket. He was so exhausted at the end of the day that he "could scarcely crawl to the surface. I reeled as one

The original Vertin Brothers Department Store in Calumet, before the addition of the two upper stories. Credit: Keweenaw Digital Archives, Michigan Technological University Archives and Copper Country Historical Collections, Houghton, MI.

drunk." After three days, however, he was used to the tedium and incredibly taxing labor, especially since he had new callouses to protect his hands and feet. Even so, he feared for his safety, although people told him that he had nothing to be afraid of. In particular, he singled out the trammers as having the most dangerous job—masses of rock could crush them at any time. He witnessed more than one such accident.

"Peda," or payday, was always a cause for celebration. After his first month, Molek received sixty-two dollars. After paying off the advance given him for travel and clothing, he had little left. However, he was, for the first time since leaving Slovenia, "free from the worry of unemployment."[98] Even though he had little left, he witnessed the holiday atmosphere that surrounded payday. Saloons and taverns anticipated increased business and stocked up accordingly. On the Saturday after they received their pay, Slovenes paid off debts, sent some money back to Slovenia, and tried to have a good time. The saloons played music from the old country, and dancing was encouraged. Molek also stated that prostitution was present, but many of those transactions occurred outside of the city limits.

Molek took note of how his situation had changed since he left Pennsylvania. He had steady work, and the pay was higher, but room and board were also higher, as was the cost of food and clothing. He noted that beer cost the same, but the glasses were smaller. While he missed the sun, the Slovene community ties were strong, and Molek truly enjoyed that. He stated,

> But I had progressed socially. The new community: compact, full of talented, interesting characters with whom I associated pleasurably . . . There were many opportunities for relaxation, self-education and healthful entertainment, more than in a great many other places in the United States.[99]

Molek had family outside of Calumet as well. One Sunday he visited a farm near Torch Lake with his uncle and cousin. Another aunt, uncle, and cousin farmed there, and along the way he saw, for the first time, other structures associated with mining, along with the brown water byproduct that was the result of smelting and refining. While he visited his extended family, he learned that a man named Frank Jutrazh lived in the town of Laurium. Jutrazh's father had been mayor of Metlika, the town in Slovenia that Molek hailed from.

After a time, Molek decided to take up the offer he had received and started to write pieces for the Slovene newspaper. That caused friction with his family, as they accused him of taking too much time writing. After he complained that he had little room to write, his uncle told him that he could find lodging elsewhere, which he ultimately did. The more he wrote, the happier Molek was. In addition, he suffered a mining injury when a car filled with rock rolled over the top of him and ripped the flesh on his hip and elbow to the bone. The accident caused him to lose all interest in mining, and luckily a new opportunity arose. A man named Frank Petrich, a representative from the Slovene newspaper that was printed in Chicago, visited Calumet. Molek left Calumet on May 1, 1905, to travel to Chicago to edit the *Glas Svobode*.[100] While his time in the Copper Country was short, his writings provide a treasure trove of insights into the lives of the Slovene immigrants who lived in the region. His stories were corroborated by and added to by others in later years.

Slovenes Remember: Oral Histories

During his tenure at Northern Michigan University, professor Russell Magnaghi oversaw the creation of a vast oral history library. He conducted hundreds of interviews and trained scores of students in the pedagogy of oral history. Some of those interviews were with Slovenes. Their memories further enrich the narrative of Slovene life in Michigan.

Frank Plautz was the son of Slovene immigrants in Calumet. His grandfather was Joseph Plavec—the Slovene spelling of the name—and his father was John.[101] His grandfather was trained as a veterinarian in Slovenia and went to Mexico, where he barely avoided being executed as part of an uprising. He then made his way to America and ultimately to Copper Country. John Plautz worked at the Vertin Brother's store and had also worked for the Slovene newspaper. Ivan Molek remarked that he became best friends with Plautz while he lived in Calumet.[102]

Frank Plautz provided excellent insights into Slovene life, and immigrant life in general, in the Upper Peninsula. The unnamed interviewer started by asking Plautz to talk about Croatian life in the Copper Country. Plautz quickly reminded him that they would be discussing *Slovene* culture and explained that there was always a great deal of rivalry and mutual contempt for people who lived close together in Europe. This was particularly true between Slovenes and Croatians, although he referred to Serbians as "the real animals." Yugoslavia was not a natural ethnic grouping; different ethnicities were pushed together. A mere river separates Slovenia and Croatia, but there were tensions that spilled into the Copper Country. The Slovene were seen as cultural elitists and as "a bunch of snobs" by the Croatians. Interestingly, and not confined to the Copper Country, while the local Slovene and Croatian populations shared tensions, they also shared a common religion: Roman Catholicism. Plautz also stated that this was true of many groups who lived close together in Europe, such as the rivalry between Finns, Norwegians, and Swedes.[103]

Language and education were important to Plautz and his parents. His maternal family settled in Manistique originally and worked as lumberjacks. His paternal side settled in Calumet, with its larger Slovene community. Like many immigrants, they hoped to get rich quickly and return home. In addition, many men left Europe to avoid conscription in armies and became American citizens.

Finishing grade school was a luxury for immigrants, since they had to start work so young. Undaunted, Plautz's parents continued to educate themselves once their formal school ended. His mother could speak Slovene fluently but was unable to read or write it. She refused to lose her language, so she taught herself to read and write in her native tongue. In fact, Plautz recalled that most South Slavic immigrants picked up each other's languages with relative ease, despite the differences. He stated that they were not having intensive "philosophical dialogues," but in daily conversations, they did quite well.

Plautz described a variety of Slovene cultural characteristics. He said that Slovene ideals from the old country perpetuated in Michigan and centered on the church and holidays. Food was a major part of that, because for a people who were otherwise quite poor, food was a major source of pleasure and pride. Easter was more important than Christmas overall.

In order to prepare for the long winters, barrels of sauerkraut were prepared, along with approximately fifteen bushels of apples and thirty bushels of potatoes. Carrots and turnips were stored in boxes of sand, and families enjoyed homemade wine. Gardens were as large as possible, and Slovene families had gardens on their own property and often leased other land as well.

Plautz felt that Slovenes were much more culturally orientated than other immigrant groups, a point that certainly is up for serious debate. He stated that education and music were vital to the culture, and at the time of the interview (likely in the early 1980s), there was an active Slovene Opera Company in the United States.[104]

• • •

Another interview from the Central Upper Peninsula and Northern Michigan University Archives was conducted with Anna Murvich in 1983. She was born in Calumet on November 28, 1915. While many of her statements echo those of Plautz, a key difference was the fact that her parents, both immigrants from Slovenia, never had any desire to return to their home country. She stated that they were "fiercely proud" of being American.[105] She also started the interview by cutting off the interviewer's questions and explaining that, in order to begin, she needed to provide a description of Slovenia, since no one knows where it is. Many Slovene immigrants, she stated, came because the land in the old country goes to the oldest son, which seriously inhibits the options of other siblings. Many Slovenes came to the Copper Country and wrote glowing reports of the opportunities available.[106] That did not mean that there was not some amount of culture shock. Murvich related a story that her mother told her about the first glimpse she had of Calumet when she arrived. She told her daughter that in Slovenia, the homes were constructed out of stone and brick and tended to be bright. All of the homes she saw in Michigan were dark wooden structures, some made of logs. She wondered if she had been duped. Where were the streets paved in gold and the land of plenty?

Unlike Plautz, Murvich mentioned the Ruppe and Vertin families, as well as Bishop Frederic Baraga. She felt that, in 1983, the cause of Baraga's canonization was progressing well, and that he brought a number of other Slovenes to the United States to serve as priests. The other prominent Copper Country Slovenes, the Ruppe and Vertin families, owned grocery and department stores, and she recalled that "one of their sons" was a bishop. Another Slovene family named Grichar owned a grocery store.

Many of the Slovene cultural traditions Murvich recalled were similar to those Plautz shared. Murvich also pointed out that many other ethnicities had similar customs. For example, many women served as workers in boarding houses, and taverns were considered social hubs. New insights she provided included a number of traditional Slovene recipes, which are shared later in this work. There were unique "Austrian" sausages that were nearly a foot in length and must be smoked. She also remembered the gardens—the more the better— they had in their own yards and that they leased "potato lots" from others.

After she finished school, Murvich worked as a secretary for the Calumet & Hecla Mining Company. When it closed, she worked at Michigan Technological University as a secretary and then earned a degree in liberal arts from that institution. Not long before she granted this interview, she visited a Slovene hall in Detroit. At one point the master of ceremonies asked where everyone was from. Murvich claimed that nearly everyone in the room was either directly from Calumet or descended from those who originally settled in Calumet. She remembered mass exoduses from the Copper Country due to strikes, particularly in the 1920s.

Taken together, the information provided by Molek, Plautz, and Murvich illustrate a cross section of Slovene life in Michigan. It also illustrates the relative paucity of information available on many of these topics. They all provided information on a subject that many more sources are available for: religion.

Slovene Catholic Communities in the Copper Country: St. Joseph Catholic Church

A Slovene priest, Joseph Zalokar, helped found the church that was dedicated to St. Joseph by Bishop Vertin on November 29, 1889. The Slovenes built their church on land leased from a mining company on the corner of Oak and Eighth Streets in Calumet. A great deal of money was rapidly raised to help construct the building. After a two thousand-dollar donation was received, a one-day fundraising effort raised an additional six thousand dollars. The first marriage celebrated in the wooden structure was between George Mischa and Katherine Zapancic on May 23, 1889.[107] A second Slovene priest, Rev. Mark Pakiz, arrived in 1891 and remained until 1904. After his arrival, the parish prepared to open a parish school as well but disaster struck. On December 9, 1902, a fire destroyed the church. While they reconstructed their burned church, the Slovenes celebrated mass at St. Mary's, the Catholic church that the Italian immigrants used.[108]

Raising money for the grand church that the Slovenes envisioned was a difficult undertaking. Frank Plautz recalled that money came from both the Upper Peninsula and from Slovenes in the old country. Anna Murvich confirmed what the *Daily Mining Gazette* reported—Slovene families were expected to contribute eighty-five dollars each, and single men were to contribute fifty dollars each. In fact, she stated that the bachelors of the congregation were thanked for paying for the organ by a plaque. The organ was impressive and consisted of 962 pedals, and accompanied a choir that was composed entirely of Slovenes and was reputed to be the best in the Copper Country. There were 350 Slovene families in the parish and over four hundred single men. As the cornerstone for the new building was being laid on August 18, 1903, women parishioners held concerts, plays, and other fundraisers to buy the altar. Ivan Molek thought that the costs associated with the new church bordered on the absurd. The building alone cost over $46,000, and he estimated that the entire project could cost over $100,000. He felt that there was no need for such a magnificent structure and that the Slovenes of Calumet were competing with the Slovene community in Joliet, Illinois.[109] Regardless, a building committee consisted of a number of prominent Slovenes, including the Vertin brothers, Peter Ruppe, and John Plautz.

Bishop Frederick Eis dedicated the new church on June 18, 1908. The priest in charge of the new church was Luke Klopic, a Slovene who took over for Father Pakiz in 1904. He remained in his post until 1932.[110] Officers of the church included both Vertin brothers as secretary and treasurer. Polish Catholics joined the parish when their own closed due to dwindling numbers after the copper strikes in 1913. The parish continued to thrive into the 1920s, when a new rectory was added. Father Klopic went to Slovenia in 1930, the same year a centennial celebration for Bishop Baraga was celebrated. Klopic passed away in 1932, and a Slovene who had been ordained from St. Joseph's, Father Francis Scheringer, was appointed. St. Joseph's celebrated its golden jubilee in 1948 and published an accompanying booklet.[111] The booklet shows an active Slovene community, though much smaller than the heady days of the past.

In 1965, one year before a major parish consolidation, St. Joseph published a diamond jubilee program.[112] In the years proceeding that celebration, many improvements were made, including updates to the twin steeples of the building. To prepare for the jubilee, each member of the church was

St. Joseph Catholic Church, which was located on Oak Street in Calumet. This church served the Slovene community, and was later replaced by a more elaborate structure. Credit: Keweenaw Digital Archives, Michigan Technological University Archives and Copper Country Historical Collections, Houghton, MI.

asked to contribute one hundred dollars—twenty dollars each year over five years. In addition, money was contributed for a centralized Catholic school to serve the numerous Catholic parishes of the area. That school, Sacred Heart Central, a grade school, was dedicated in 1957.[113]

In 1966, due to declining numbers of both population and parishioners, and the resulting economic woes, Bishop Thomas Noa decided to combine four ethnic parishes of Calumet: French-Canadian St. Anne, Croatian St.

St. Ignatius Loyola Church

Another church in the Copper Country with deep Slovene roots is St. Ignatius Loyola Church, located in Houghton. Bishop Frederic Baraga dedicated the original church on July 31, 1859. The original building remained intact until 1902, when it was partially torn down for the construction of the current church, and the remainder of it was demolished for a garage in 1950.*

The longest-serving pastor of the church was Antoine Rezek, author of the two-volume *History of the Diocese of Sault Ste. Marie and Marquette*. He served from 1895–1946. He oversaw the construction of the current church, which was dedicated on August 10, 1902.† The church prospered as well as it could through the declining numbers that all Catholic parishes experienced throughout the mid to late twentieth century. In 1988 the interior was completely restored and was rededicated in July of that year. The members of the church raised over $350,000 for the restoration.‡

**Daily Mining Gazette*, November 18, 1950.

†Angela S. Johnson, *Seasons of Faith: A Walk through the History of the Roman Catholic Diocese of Marquette, 1900–2000* (Marquette, MI: Roman Catholic Diocese of Marquette, 2006), 185.

‡Copper Country Vertical File, Michigan Technological University Archives, Houghton, MI.

John, the Italian St. Mary, and the Slovene St. Joseph. The Slovene church, St. Joseph, was chosen to be the site of the new consolidated parish that was dedicated to St. Paul the Apostle. In 1987 the building was named a Michigan Historic Site. The original organ that the Slovene bachelor's paid for in 1908 remains in use.[114]

Fraternal Benefit Societies

Another aspect of community that Slovenes participated in was the creation of fraternal benefit societies. The first Slovene fraternal society was established in Calumet. Until 1882, most Slovenes were members of a German fraternal society since they lacked one of their own. These societies were important since most mining companies felt no duty to compensate their workers for injuries or their families for death. The lodge, St. Joseph's, was established on September 17, 1882.[115] Eighty members signed the charter, and the benefits were set at fifty cents each sick day. If a member died, the surviving members each contributed one dollar to the family of the deceased.[116] These organizations played a crucial role in Slovene life. There were no safety nets for workers or their families, and these societies helped fill that void. Given the dangerous nature of mining work, the measures provided were all the more important.[117] Frank Plautz recalled that his father was active in the lodge and that they were "clannish, and distrustful of American insurance."[118]

The Slovenes in the Copper Country set up a number of other fraternal benefit societies that were modeled after the lodge of St. Joseph's. They included

1. Slovenian Roman Catholic Benefit Society of St. Peter No. 30, associated on June 7, 1899, in Calumet, to "Provide for the relief of needy and distressed members, the visitation of the sick, the burial of the dead, and such other benevolent fund worthy purposes and objects as effect the members of the corporation and others. Members must talk and read the Slovenian language, be a Roman Catholic, and pass a satisfactory medical examination."
2. St. Cirila in Metoda Society of Calumet, Michigan, associated on August 25, 1901, to "Provide for the relief of needy and distressed members, the visitation of the sick, the burial of the dead, and such other benevolent and worthy purposes and objects as effect the members of the corporation and others. Qualification: Any man who is a Slavonian [*sic*] and a citizen of the state of MI (pay dues)."
3. Slovenic Croatian Union, associated on May 17, 1906, to "Improve the moral, mental, social, and physical condition of its members, to aid, assist, and support them, or their families in case of want, sickness, accident, disability, or death, and to create, hold, manage, and disburse a fund for the relief of such members and their families only and not for profit, in the case of want, sickness, accident, disability, or death by payment of benefits by assessments levied upon such members. Also be a lodge system with ritualistic work and a representative form of government. Qualifications: US and Canadian residents and of South Slavic descent, ages 16–45, said age limit to be subject to further restrictions within said limits by the constitution or by-laws, and applicants for life benefits shall be required to undergo satisfactory medical examination."

4. St. Matijas Society of Baltic, Michigan, associated on May 1, 1909, to "promote friendship and charity among its members, to help and assist them in sickness and distress, to give them such pecuniary benefit as the Society may see fit, and aid their survivors or heirs after death of a deceased member, and to give a proper burial to all its deceased members. Qualifications: Residents of Houghton County, Officers must be US and Michigan residents, must be a male and must be a Slovenian or Croatian by birth or descent, must be a member of the Roman Catholic Church, cannot belong to any Society or organization condemned by the Church, nor to any professing or teaching socialistic doctrines, or which is in any way connected with socialism. Must be 18–45 to apply, and pass physical examination. Must receive communion once every year."
5. Slovenian Young Men's Union of St. Aloysius, associated on October 29, 1909, to "Provide relief for the needy and distressed members, visitation of the sick, burial of the dead and such other benevolent and worthy purposes and objects as effect the members of the Corporation and others. Qualifications: Single men between 16 and 40 years old of Slovenian and Croatian nationality, and married men of Slovenian origin only, that married since the year 1904, and all members must be Roman Catholic faith, and not a member of any Anti Catholic Society, and of good character and reputation, and shall pass a medical examination."[119]

Women also started organizations of their own. The Marijina Druzba, later renamed the Altar Society, began in 1894. The Corpus Christi Court of the Women's Catholic Order of Foresters was organized in 1900 and was the first Slovene lodge for women in the Copper Country. The Slovenian Ladies Union was organized in 1929.[120]

The benefit societies did not operate in theory only; with the dangerous nature of mining work, they were called upon more than once to pay out benefits. According to the Houghton County Mine Inspector's Report, a Slovene named John Pirc was killed on April 29, 1908, in the Number Fourteen Shaft of the Calumet & Hecla Mine. Witnesses stated that the accident occurred around 7:30 A.M. While no one actually saw anything, they heard a sound of something falling and considered the possibility that someone dumped a cart over. Apparently Pirc had crossed a shaft and fallen to his death about thirty feet below. Interestingly, both witnesses who testified

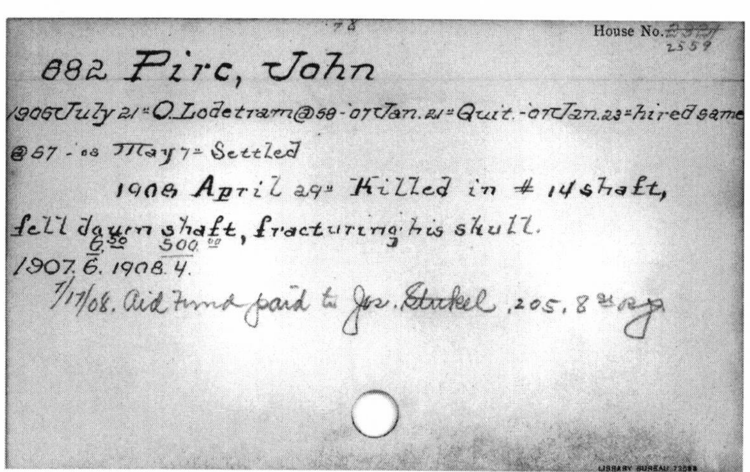
House No. 2559

882 Pirc, John

1906 July 21 = O. Lodetram @58 - '07 Jan. 21 = Quit. - '07 Jan. 23 = hired same

@57 - '08 May 7 = Settled

1908 April 29 = Killed in #14 shaft,

fell down shaft, fracturing his skull.

6.50 500.00

1907. 6. 1908. 4.

7/17/08. Aid fund paid to Jos. Stukel, 205. 8

The employment record of Slovene John Pirc, who was killed in an accident at the Calumet & Hecla Mine on April 29, 1908. Credit: Keweenaw Digital Archives, Michigan Technological University Archives and Copper Country Historical Collections, Houghton, MI.

used the same language, perhaps to alleviate responsibility away from the company and the hazardous conditions of the work: "He did not need to cross the shaft to his work."[121]

In addition to the financial benefits that these organizations provided, there was a sense of Slovene community present as well. Ivan Molek described the ample entertainment that was available because of the benevolent and social lodges. Those groups, he said, "every Sunday, conducted picnics or outings in the nearby wooded area; and there was no beginning nor end to drinking and devouring."[122]

Slovenes Across the Upper Peninsula

The heartland of Slovene immigration was the Copper Country, with over 1,500 first-generation immigrants living there in 1910. The next largest Slovene community was located in Gogebic County, which numbered nearly four hundred. They were attracted to that area by the work available in the iron mines of Ironwood, Bessemer, and Wakefield.

In other parts of the Upper Peninsula, Slovenes found jobs in the woods

Traunik

While the Copper Country by far held the largest concentration of Slovenes in Michigan, that did not mean that there were no other pockets around. The records are difficult to come by, or, in the words of one scholar who attempted to piece together the history of Slovenes elsewhere in the Upper Peninsula, "practically non-existent."* One exception is the village of Traunik, which was founded in 1906. The name Traunik comes directly from a region in Slovenia by the same name, where a number of Slovenes had roots. The Slovenes who settled there came from Cleveland, home of a large Slovene community. The Cleveland Cliffs Iron Company recruited lumbermen from that area to work in the Upper Peninsula. Once Slovenes arrived, they turned lumber camps into more permanent settlements and cleared land for farming, with dairy cows and potatoes as the mainstays.

Traunik counted five hundred inhabitants at its peak in the 1930s.† Even the remote location did not inhibit the Slovenes from keeping their traditional culture. They celebrated weddings over a period of days. Foods like potica and felina were served at holidays, as was porbiks, which is made of beans, noodles, and gravy.‡ While men cut wood, women worked at home, farmed, and took on jobs as housekeepers, where they were paid ten dollars a month.

In 1927, the village grew to the point of needing a post office. The village had a "business district," with a tavern, warehouse, grocery store, and Traunik Hall, the community focal point. A chapter of the Slovene National Benefit Society was started as well and served a social function, much like similar groups in the Copper Country.§

After World War II, the town started to decline. Veterans wanted an easier life than farming afforded, and farms and Traunik Hall fell into disrepair. Even so, the village endures today, and an original structure, Mikulich's Grocery Store, remains. Today it is under non-Slovene ownership and is a general store and restaurant.

*George P. Graff, "Traunik, Michigan—A Slovenian Community in Alger County," (unpublished manuscript, Marquette County Historical Society, 1970).

†Barbara McCann, "Women of Traunik: A Story of Slovenian Immigration," *Michigan History* 68, no. 1 (January/February 1984), 41–45.

‡Graff, "Traunik, Michigan."

§See McCann, "Women of Traunik."

as lumbermen. This was isolated and dangerous work, and was seasonal in nature. Many others found work in saw and paper mills in Manistique. There were also chemical plants that processed charcoal.

While the majority of Slovene immigrants were attracted to the mining areas and their respective materials, a small number of them attempted farming. Nearly a dozen Slovene farmers had built large-scale agriculture operations by the spring of 1910.[123]

Slovene Exodus from the Copper Country

In the Lower Peninsula a number of Slovene immigrants got into framing, but they remained a minority. The bulk of their number sought employment in mining and manufacturing. One group of farmers settled in Wexford County in 1912, and by 1910 there were over thirty farmers. One of them, Michael Krully, first settled in the western United States as a miner but then decided to try his hand in farming. Others worked as laborers in sugar beet production in Tuscola County and Bay County. In the western part of the peninsula, some tried their luck farming a variety of berries and vegetables.

A number of factors attracted Slovenes to Metro Detroit, Flint, Pontiac, and Ann Arbor. Foremost was the booming automobile industry. In addition, a major strike hit the copper industry in the Upper Peninsula between 1913–14. Other incidents, including the Barnes-Hecker disaster in 1926 and the fact that copper demand declined after World War I caused a number of Slovenes to chase their fortunes elsewhere. Some went to other states with sizable Slovene populations, including Illinois, Pennsylvania, and Ohio. Others decided to remain in Michigan and tried their hands in Detroit.

In the summer of 1927, Ivan Molek revisited Calumet, more than twenty years after he left. He was astonished by what he found. He estimated that the population was one-third what it had been in the early part of the century. Once thriving, the copper mines were "scarcely alive." Molek blamed the strike for the loss of many landmarks and buildings that he remembered, including the location of the Slovene newspaper and Klobuchar's Tavern. His old friend John J. Plautz, father of Frank Plautz, still lived there and showed him the network of roads that connected the communities of the area. He stated that they drove in an hour what used to take a day by horse, "a demonstration of how the Copper Country had shrunk within the last twenty years." He visited Calumet eight more times during his life, and each time the numbers of people he encountered and remembered, as well as the populations of the towns, dwindled.[124]

Slovenes in Detroit

Like so many other immigrant groups, the Slovenes that moved to Detroit generally settled together. They chose the suburb of Highland Park to congregate, and their social, religious, and cultural lives centered around a Catholic church. The first Slovene in Detroit was Joseph Faletich, who arrived in 1903 and opened a saloon.[125] More arrived to work in the automotive industry. In the early 1920s, those newly arrived immigrants attended services at the Croatian parish, St. Jerome. However, the Slovene community missed having a priest preaching in their native tongue. By the middle of the 1920s, a group of men including Louis Srebernak, Peter Zunich, and Frank Pavlich took upon themselves the task of funding a Slovene church. They formally placed a request before the Catholic hierarchy in Detroit in 1925. In 1926, a Slovene priest from Illinois embarked upon a mission trip to St. Jerome to conduct mass in Slovene. This was the catalyst for the ultimate founding of a Slovene parish, which would be named St. John Vianney.[126]

During the visit of the Slovene priest from Illinois, a ladies group called the "Good Intention Society" was formed and was quite influential in establishing the new parish. Once St. John Vianney was founded, the group renamed itself the "Rosary Altar Society." The year 1926 is regarded by some as the official birth of the parish, as the first baptism was performed on November 13, when Mildred Babich received the sacrament.[127] However, the bishop did not issue his formal letter of erection for the new church until July 1927.[128] The permanent location of the parish was on the corner of Geneva Avenue and Twelfth Street. As early as April 1926 the bishop granted permission for property to be purchased for a new church and to have an architect sketch some designs. The cost of the endeavor was over $20,000.[129] By July twelve Slovene men were named to the committee of the young parish.[130] Four names were submitted to Bishop Gallagher of Detroit: Jesus Christ King, Holy Ghost, Blessed Lady of Help, and St. John Vianey [*sic*], with the stipulation that "the first one would be preferred."[131]

While the particulars were being ironed out, a more fundamental problem presented itself: where to locate a permanent Slovene-speaking priest. Salvation came from the same group that sent the original missionary to the area earlier in 1926, the Franciscan Fathers of the Commissariat of the Holy Cross, located in Lemont, Illinois. The correspondence relating to this also illustrates that the Slovene Catholics in Michigan were not immune to the fundamentalist impulses swirling around the United States during the 1920s, which included anti-Catholic sentiments. In a letter to Bishop Gallagher, Kazimir Zakrajsek, a leading member of the Franciscans in Lemont, mentioned that the report Father Bernard Ambrozic delivered stated that he felt that "something more ought to be done for them in order to not allow the anti-Catholic agitators to posing their minds entirely and pull them away from religion."[132] Zakrajsek felt that the best way to save the Slovenes from that poison was to establish their own parish. The Franciscans were willing to send someone to preach in Slovene, but only if Detroit fully committed. Bishop Gallagher agreed and stated that he was "very grateful that Father Bernard is getting along so well in organizing a Slovenian Parish in our city, and thereby taking care of a most urgent need. I will also be very grateful if you see your way clear to leave him in Detroit continually, or as near so as possible."[133] With a Slovene priest in place, a commitment from the Bishop of Detroit, and a site chosen, St. John Vianney was established.

By late 1930, an unexpected issue arose when the original pastor, Bernard Ambrozic, was transferred to Chicago. The trouble stemmed from the new priest, Rev. Pascal Esser, a Franciscan who had assisted Ambrozic at St. John Vianney prior to the latter's departure for Chicago. He had been well received by the parish initially. However, a number of Slovenes were appalled at Esser's use of English for certain services, which even Ambrozic

Exterior of St. John Vianney Catholic Church in Highland Park. The parish served the Slovene population of the area. Credit: St. John Vianney Highland Park Parish Collection, Archives of the Archdiocese of Detroit.

admitted to doing "for the benefit of our young generation and others." However, certain members of St. John Vianney accused Esser of "killing the Slovenian language." When word about what was happening in his former church reached him, Ambrozic wrote to Bishop Gallagher: "There is a trouble in the Parish of St. John Vianney in Detroit."[134] While Ambrozic did not agree with the assessment of what he considered "several narrow-minded parishioners," he felt that he had to respond to numerous requests to have Esser removed from the church. A Slovene weekly newspaper, with a circulation of approximately 25,000, published an article about the situation that stated that according to Ambrozic, his successor was "killing the language of his parishioners and his person is alleged as an obstacle to the progress of the Congregation." As a result, Esser resigned, and Ambrozic recommended that the Franciscans abandon St. John Vianney.[135] In response to the situation, the committee members of the parish wrote to Bishop Gallagher to assure him that the majority of those who attended St. John Vianney were satisfied with the Franciscans and that it was only a small minority of parishioners who caused the disturbance. They further stated that they "humbly beg of you to leave the Franciscans with us and keep the present Fathers too."[136] The correspondence grows silent as to what happened next, save for a response from Gallagher to Ambrozic that included a copy of the petition from the committee members, which to Gallagher meant that the situation was not as bad as it first seemed.[137]

Perhaps part of the blame for the unsettled state of affairs stemmed from the fact that the parish did not yet have a final home. Although money had been set aside for land purchases and architects contacted as early as 1926, the permanent church was not dedicated until July 9, 1933. On that date, both Bishop Gallagher and Father Ambrozic celebrated mass, with Ambrozic speaking in Slovene. Up until that date, the parishioners of St. John Vianney celebrated mass in a number of temporary facilities, including schools and a Knights of Columbus hall. With a final home erected, the members of the parish focused their energies on growth.[138]

The years of the Great Depression saw the Slovene parish struggle with the same issues that all Americans faced, but the parish seemed to remain in solid financial standing. In 1937, structural problems were discovered in a facility that they used for hall purposes that necessitated its destruction, and a new boiler for heat was needed in the new church. The heating situation then in place was described as such: "The church is nothing less than frigid." In a letter to the chancery office, Rev. Augustine Svete wrote, "Financially speaking, the church is safe–being without debt."[139] It is truly amazing that even during the throes of the Great Depression, the support and dedication of the members of this church was unwavering. During World War II, the parish continued to grow, and the church remained fiscally sound. and the parish purchased additional lots to construct a parochial school. Although land for a school was purchased in 1942, it would be several years before the school came to fruition.[140] In the meantime, a number of groups started. Unfortunately, there are no minutes or other documentation as to what all these different groups accomplished, but a glance at their membership numbers shows a dedicated and thriving church. For example, the National Council of Catholic Women had seventy-one members, the Holy Name Society had forty-five members, and the Order of St. Francis had 125 members. In addition, an annual report mentioned, "Though surrounded by non-Catholics unfavorable to the Catholic Church." As of 1940, the parish census tallied ninety Slovene families and 140 "mixed" families, or families with both Catholic and non-Catholic members.[141] By 1948, the census indicated that there were 1200 total members, with eighty Slovene families.[142]

As St. John Vianney approached its Silver Jubilee, things continued to go well, although the number of Slovene members started to dwindle, especially as people of that ethnicity aged. In 1951 the ecumenical status of the parish was changed to territorial, which provided for specific boundaries. In the letter that informed Rev. Thomas Hoge of this change, the vice chancellor stipulated that, "I am confident that those elderly people of Slovenian descent who belong to other parishes in the city will encounter no difficulty with their proper pastor in arranging, if they wish, to continue to frequent St. John Vianney's."[143] While their numbers may have decreased, the Slovenes who remained near Highland Park and St. John Vianney parish clung tenaciously to their church. They also embraced their new members with open arms with the new status of the parish.

A primary concern with the establishment of St. John Vianney as a territorial parish was education. The neighborhood was established and settled, and finding a location for a school was a challenge. They looked to available land parcels to combine with land that had been purchased previously. Architect Walter J. Rozycki designed the school at a cost of approximately $225,000. Groundbreaking ceremonies were conducted in March of 1952, with a projected opening that fall. However, labor strikes pushed that back, and the school was not opened until 1955. Sisters of the Immaculate Heart of Mary took up teaching duties, spread amongst three sisters and one lay teacher, and 134 students enrolled throughout seven grade levels.[144]

By the early summer of 1978, it was clear that St. John Vianney was doomed. The last annual report available was 1977. It listed just 125 souls and even mentioned that the parish might have to close.[145] On June 30, Archbishop John Cardinal Dearden received a letter from the Franciscan Fathers who had provided priests to St. John Vianney since its inception that stated that, "It is my sad duty to inform you that at our custodial board meeting on June 27th 1978 it was decided that we, the Franciscans will withdraw from St. John Vianney in Highland Park."[146] There were no scandals or personal reasons associated with the decision; a shortage of priests was the issue at hand. Sometime between the end of June and the end of August the decision was made and announced that the Archdiocese of Detroit was going to close St. John Vianney. A church that had Slovene roots had grown into something much greater. A number of black individuals and families attended the church over its existence as well. One of them, a woman named Valerie Holland, wrote an impassioned letter begging that the Archdiocese do something to keep a small but vitally important parish open.[147] However, the decision had been made and was finalized on September 26, 1978, when Archbishop Dearden issued a decree that suppressed the church, to take "effect immediately."[148]

Although their parish closed, Slovenes remained in the area. However, the record thins considerably. A study prepared by the Michigan Ethnic Heritage Studies Center and the University of Michigan in 1983 sheds light on what happened to Slovenes in Detroit after the closure of St. John Vianney. They found eight thousand Slovenes in Michigan at that time, of whom four thousand lived in Detroit. There were two lodges, one of which, the Slovene American Club, still exists. However, the study mentioned the fact that a "stalemate of activities occurred among the Slovenes in Detroit when the younger set was unsuccessful in establishing and maintaining a viable youth group."[149] In addition, as Detroit Slovenes aged, they moved to warmer climates. The decline continues today. In 2015, the newsletter of the Slovene American Club in Melvindale, Michigan, listed a number of activities that had to be cancelled to due low participation, and the hall fears that unless things improve, they will have to close.

Conclusion

While the stories presented earlier are the best documented, there were other pockets of Slovene immigrants in Michigan, including in Flint and in Oceana County.[150] In the Upper Peninsula, the 1910 Census, which actually lists Slovenes separately, shows sizable numbers of them in Alger, Dickinson, Gogebic, Iron, Keweenaw, and Schoolcraft counties, working in a variety of occupations, but mainly as miners, laborers, and lumbermen.

Once-thriving locales of Slovene activities, such as Calumet, are a mere shadow of their former grandeur. Even those cities with larger populations, including Flint and Detroit, do not resemble what early Slovenes encountered. In his interview, Frank Plautz wrestled with the question, "What happened to the Slovene population?" He recalled that once they had their own newspaper, but now their communities were difficult to find. To him, had the mines remained open, that would not have happened. In addition, Plautz felt that the melting pot worked and assimilation occurred. While some traditions were kept, especially food, proceeding generations lost more and more of what it means to be Slovene. Finally, he blamed intermarriage between ethnicities: "It strips away identity."

The descendants of some of the biggest names in Michigan Slovene history echo through the ages. Over one hundred years after his ancestors arrived in the Copper Country, another John Vertin was present when the department store his family still ran celebrated its one hundred-year anniversary in 1985. He was noted for being a major civil leader, and open-heart surgery did not slow down his sixty-hour workweeks.[151] Prior to that, the Vertin family was awarded the Distinguished Family Award Leaders in Retail. As late as 1999, the *Daily Mining Gazette* printed a message entitled "Thank You John."

Descendants of another Calumet pioneer, Peter Ruppe, were well known in politics. Philip Ruppe was born in Laurium in 1926 and served in the United States House of Representatives from 1967 to 1979. His wife, Loret, served as the United States ambassador to Norway and directed the Peace Corps from 1981 to 1989. During George H. W. Bush's presidential campaign, the *Detroit News* published an article that listed her as a possible vice presidential candidate. She died of ovarian cancer at the age of sixty.[152]

Legacy of Frederic Baraga

Frederic Baraga continues to be quite popular with Catholics, particularly in the Upper Peninsula and to those of Slovene heritage. The Upper Peninsula is home to the town of Baraga and Baraga County, many Baraga Streets and Avenues, a sixty-foot-foot bronze shrine in addition to numerous smaller ones, and Baraga Park. The Baraga home is in Cleveland, Ohio, and the Baraga Pilgrimage Home is located in Lemont, Illinois. Internationally there is a Baraga Mission Center in Buenos Aires, the Baraga House for Immigrants in Australia, and the Baraga Theological Seminary in Ljubljana.[153]

Many Catholics consider Frederic Baraga a saint, even without the authorization of the Vatican. The Bishop Baraga Association was founded in Chicago in 1930 to promote the cause of Baraga's canonization. Marquette Bishop Thomas Noa officially opened the cause in 1952. In 1972 Joseph Gregorich presented the Vatican Congregation of Causes for Sainthood with fourteen volumes that documented Baraga's life, deeds, and purported intercessions. Several miracles have been proposed to date, but none have withstood the Vatican's scrutiny.

Baraga was the first in an impressive procession of Slovenes to come to North America for missionary work. He regularly wrote letters and reports to Europe about the need for priests and went on two recruiting trips. In

Members of the Singing Slovenes perform at the annual Bishop Baraga Days celebration in 2013. Credit: Tom Buchkoe and the Bishop Baraga Association, Marquette, MI.

her dissertation, Maureen Anna Harp states that the twenty-some Slovene priests who followed Baraga in the Great Lakes "did work for some time with the Ottawa and Ojibwa(y), bringing to bear the greatest single ethnic Catholic influence on the Native Americans in this region in the nineteenth century."[154]

Francis Pierz, Otto Skolla, and Joseph Buh are among those who answered the call when the shortage of priests put Catholics in the Upper Peninsula into dire straits. Buh responded to Pierz's appeal for additional priests and arrived in the United States in 1864. He worked in Minnesota for the remainder of his life. Like Baraga, both Pierz and Buh wrote about Native Americans.[155] In addition, the two bishops of the Diocese of Sault Sainte Marie and Marquette who came after Baraga—Mrak and Vertin—were Slovene.[156]

The Slovene missionaries who worked with the Ojibwa utilized a conversion process different from their fellow Protestant missionaries. They did not expect comprehension of Catholic doctrine from the Native Americans. There is evidence that the Eucharist, among other aspects, was glossed over or not taught at all out of a fear that Native Americans would equate it with cannibalism. Protestants spent much more time educating Native Americans about Christian beliefs. For most of them, baptism was the final step. Catholics saw baptism as one of many steps toward salvation, although it appears that as long as Native Americans were baptized and occasionally listened to God's word, they were considered converted.[157]

Perhaps the most enduring example of Slovene culture in Michigan in the twenty-first century surrounds the support for Bishop Frederic Baraga's canonization cause, which has been ongoing for decades. It is a testament to the patience of Slovenes, as Baraga's countrymen from Michigan, elsewhere in the United States, and Slovenia continue to send money for the cause. Each year, an annual Baraga Days is held in the Great Lakes regions, and a few hundred pilgrims spend a weekend celebrating his life. On May 10, 2012, Pope Benedict XVI declared Baraga venerable, the first step toward canonization. In order for beatification to occur, the Vatican must recognize a miracle. The Bishop Baraga Association posted a message on their website that stated, "The Vatican's medical commission met on March 5, 2015 to review the potential miracle . . . They did not receive a clear majority."[158] For the faithful, it does not matter. The canonization will eventually occur. In the meantime, Slovenes in Michigan will continue to celebrate their history and heritage, with Bishop Frederic Baraga as their example. He is a vital piece in the overall picture that is the Slovene experience in Michigan.

Appendix 1

Inventory of Bishop Frederic Baraga's Assets, November 27, 1875

Location	Asset	Value (dollars)
Marquette	4 acres of land for Cemetery	50
Marquette	4 Lots and Church	5,000
Negaunee	Various land parcels	100
Negaunee	1 Lot with foundation laid for church	1,000
Michilimakinac [*sic*]	A lot with an old church and House	200
Michilimakinac [*sic*]	An old cemetery now in use	50
Point St. Ignace	A Lot with a church and Cemetery	200
Houghton	Lot, Church, and Cemetery	1,000
Hancock	2 Lots and Church House	2,000
Maple Grove	Lot & Church	300
Ontonagon	Lot, Church & Cemetery	300
Rockland	Lot, Church & Cemetery	200
Minnesota Mine	1 Acre land	60
Eagle Harbor	2 lots & church	300
Cliffs Mine	1 Acre land, Church & Cemetery	300
Wyoming	2 Lots & church	100
Sault Ste. Marie	Lot & church house	300
Sault Ste. Marie	St. Joseph's Lot & church	50

Sault Ste. Marie	St. Marie's River Indian Settlement Church	50
Ishpeming	Lot & Church	1,000
Escanaba	Lot & church	300
L'Anse	Indian Settlement, 15 acres of Land & church	200

Source: The information in this table was compiled from the Bishop Baraga Papers, Clarke Historical Library, Central Michigan University.

Appendix 2

Slovene Recipes

Potica

1½ tsp. active dry yeast
¼ cup sugar
¼ cup milk, lukewarm
1⅓ cups milk
1 cup butter, softened
1 cup butter, melted
6 egg yolks
5 cups all-purpose flour
1 tsp. salt
1 cup honey
1½ cups raisins
1½ cups chopped walnuts
1 Tbsp. ground cinnamon

Dissolve yeast, 1 teaspoon sugar, and 3 tablespoons flour in warm milk, and let stand for about 10 minutes.

In a large mixing bowl, mix together the softened butter with the remaining sugar until fluffy. Add egg yolks one at a time, and then add the yeast mixture, remaining milk, 4 cups of flour, and the salt. Mix well. Add the remaining cup of flour slowly.

Turn the dough out onto a lightly floured surface and knead for about 8 minutes. Lightly oil a bowl, add the dough, and coat with oil. Cover with a damp cloth and let rise for 60 minutes.

Lightly grease 2 cookie sheets. Punch down the dough, then divide it in half, and roll out the halves until they are about ½-inch thick. Spread each piece with the melted butter, honey, raisins, walnuts, and cinnamon. Roll up each piece and pinch the ends. Let rise again, about 45 minutes or until double in size, and preheat oven to 350°F. Bake for about 60 minutes, or until the top is golden brown.

Buckwheat Zganci

- 4 cups buckwheat flour
- 3 Tbsp. coarse wheat flour
- 6 cups of boiling water
- Salt
- Cracklings for garnish

Salt water generously and bring to a boil. Mix both flours and pour into the water. Boil until flour is submerged, then reduce the heat to low. Make a hole in the middle of the flour mixture and boil for 20 minutes. Pour some of the water out and stir well. Add the cracklings or other desired garnish, cover, and let everything rest for about 15 minutes. Crumble the zganci with a fork and serve with sauerkraut or other pickled vegetables.

Roast Sauerkraut

- 7 oz. sauerkraut
- 3½ oz. bacon
- 4¾ oz. ham
- 2 cups dry white wine
- 4 Tbsp. zaseka (minced bacon and lard or bacon jam), divided
- 1 Tbsp. peppercorns
- 1 Tbsp. juniper berries
- ½ Tbsp. caraway seeds

Preheat the oven to 350°F. Add sauerkraut and ⅔ cups water into a pan and heat to a boil. Drain any excess water, and add 2 tablespoons of zaseka or bacon jam. Place bacon slices along the bottom of a baking dish, and cover with sauerkraut. Sprinkle caraway seeds over the dish. Add ham, peppercorns, juniper berries, the remainder of the zaseka, and white wine. Bake for about 40 minutes, or until golden brown.

Cornmeal Zganci with Tomato Sauce

Tomato Sauce

1 Tbsp. canola oil
1 medium onion, finely diced
2 stalks of celery, finely diced
1 heaping Tbsp. paprika
4 cups of Roma tomatoes skins removed and diced (1½ 28-oz. cans of whole Roma tomatoes, pulsed in food processor until roughly chopped)
salt and pepper to taste
vegetable broth, warmed (optional)

In a heavy-bottomed pan, heat canola oil i over medium heat. Add the onion and sauté until translucent. Add the celery and cook until soft, then add the paprika, followed by tomatoes, salt, and pepper. Once bubbling, lower the heat and simmer the sauce gently for about 1½ hours. If the sauce starts to thicken too much, add ¼ cup of warmed vegetable broth as needed to thin it out.

Cornmeal Zganci

2 cups of cornmeal
5 cups of water
Salt to taste

Preheat oven to 350°F. Using an oven-safe pot, bring the water to a boil. Pour the cornmeal in slowly at one side of the pot. Lower the heat and let the mixture simmer gently for about 15 minutes. Do not stir. Pour some of the water, about ⅓, into a small bowl. Mix the zganci with a wooden spoon, slowly adding the reserved water until the mixture is slightly lumpy but thick. Cover with an oven-safe lid and bake for about 30–40 minutes, stirring about every 15 minutes.

Appendix 3

Institutions for Further Study

Archdiocese of Detroit Archives, 12 State Street, Detroit, MI 48266; (313) 237-5846; archives@aod.org. *Information about the Slovene parish, St. John Vianney.*

Bentley Historical Library, University of Michigan, 1150 Beal Ave., Ann Arbor, MI 48109; (734) 764-3482. *Repository of oral histories and information related to the Slovene community Traunik.*

Central Upper Peninsula and Northern Michigan University Archives, 1401 Presque Isle Ave., Marquette, MI 49855; (906) 227-1225; archives@nmu.edu. *Contains a wealth of information about Slovenes in the Upper Peninsula, including clergy, newspapers, oral histories, and vertical file information.*

Detroit Public Library, Burton Historical Collections, 5201 Woodward Ave., Detroit, MI, 48202; (313) 833-1480; bhc@detroitpubliclibrary.org. *Contains information about the Slovenes in Metro Detroit.*

Diocese of Marquette and the Bishop Baraga Association, 347 Rock Street, Marquette, MI 49855; (906) 227-9117; bishopbaraga@dioceseofmarquette.org. *Repository of records and information related to Slovene clergy, including Frederic Baraga, Ignatius Mrak, and John Vertin.*

Michigan Technological University Archives, 1400 Townsend Drive, Houghton, MI 49931; (906) 487-2505; copper@mtu.edu. *Repository of a wealth of information related to Slovenes in the Copper Country, including churches, clergy, and the Vertin and Ruppe families.*

University of Notre Dame Archives, 607 Hesburgh Library, Notre Dame, IN 46556; (574) 631-6448; archives@nd.edu. *Contains information about Frederic Baraga, including many original documents.*

Notes

1. Robert Kann and David Zdenek, *The Peoples of the Eastern Habsburg Lands, 1526–1918* (Seattle: University of Washington Press, 1984). This book is an excellent source for Slovene national history.
2. Ibid., 124.
3. Lonnie R. Johnson, *Central Europe: Enemies, Neighbors, Friends* (New York: Oxford University Press, 1996), 136–43.
4. Ibid., 329.
5. Ibid., 330, 473–75.
6. Ibid., 342.
7. Ibid., 282.
8. Ibid., 285, 293.
9. Slovenia joined the European Union on May 1, 2004.
10. Regis Walling and N. Daniel Rupp, eds., *The Diary of Bishop Frederic Baraga: First Bishop of Marquette, Michigan*, trans. Joseph Gregorich and Paul Prud'homme (Detroit: Wayne State University Press, 1990), 28; biographical information on Baraga is also available in Bernard Lambert, *Shepherd of the Wilderness: A Biography of Bishop Frederic Baraga* (Hancock, MI: Book Concern Printers, 1967); Chrysostomus P. Verwyst, *Life and Labors of Rt. Rev. Frederic Baraga, First Bishop of Marquette, Mich.* (Milwaukee: M.S. Wiltzius & Co., 1900); Joseph Gregorich, *The Apostle of the Chippewas: The Life Story of the Most Rev.*

Frederick Baraga, D.D., the First Bishop of Marquette (Chicago: Bishop Baraga Association, 1932).

11. Gregorich, *Apostle of the Chippewas*, 13.
12. Ibid., 15–22.
13. Ruth M. Murphy, "Frederic Baraga: How His Education Influenced His Mission Work in Michigan," August 1, 1985—Michigan History HS335 paper, Russell Magnaghi Papers, Central Upper Peninsula and Northern Michigan University Archives.
14. Graham A. MacDonald, trans. and ed., *Frederic Baraga's Short History of the North American Indians* (Calgary: University of Calgary Press, 2004), 8–10.
15. Gregorich, *Apostle of the Chippewas*, 27.
16. Murphy, "Frederic Baraga," 10; Gregorich, *Apostle of the Chippewas*, 33.
17. Murphy, "Frederic Baraga," 14.
18. Frederic Baraga to Amalia Baraga Gressel, August 10, 1831, Clarke Historical Library, Bishop Baraga Collection. In the same letter he recorded the Lord's Prayer in Ottawa.
19. At Harbor Springs Baraga employed a Mr. L'etourneau from Detroit to teach the sixty Native American children at the school reading, writing, arithmetic, and French. Eventually a Mrs. Fisher arrived from Mackinac to teach the girls, and Baraga spent an hour each day on religious instruction. After a while, however, L'etourneau demanded $100 per year for his work, which Baraga agreed to, because he felt the school would crumble without him. He did not, however, have access to those funds. See Frederic Baraga to Frederick Rese, November 12, 1832, Clarke Historical Library, Bishop Baraga Collection.
20. See Walter Thomas Camier, "Frederic Baraga: The Snowshoe Priest," *Crusade*, May/June 2000, 10.
21. *New Catholic Encyclopedia* (Washington, DC: Catholic University of America, 1967), 84–85.
22. Camier, "Frederic Baraga," 13. Baraga did not always have to travel alone. He chose to do so. In 1833 one of his sisters wanted to work with Baraga as a missionary. However, Baraga wrote to Frederick Rese, who had informed him that his sister Antonia was en route, that "I am not at all satisfied with her coming here. She knows not a word of French, nor will she ever learn it. Then what good can she do here?" See Frederic Baraga to Frederick Rese, March 5, 1833.
23. Throughout his life Baraga showed no tolerance for those who drank too much. Both priests and teachers suffered his fury. In 1835 he returned to a mission

station to learn that the schoolteacher had been drunk several times during his absence, and the teacher was immediately fired. Baraga also sent word to Detroit to not accept the teacher or offer him any sort of aid. Frederic Baraga to Rev. Vincent Badin, May 27, 1835, Clarke Historical Library, Bishop Baraga Collection.

24. Frederic Baraga to the Leopoldine Foundation, February 1, 1834, Clarke Historical Library, Bishop Baraga Collection.
25. Some sources list her first name as Antoinette. See Msgr F. A. O'Brien, "Lady Antoinette Von Hoeffern," *Michigan Pioneer and Historical Collections* 39 (1915): 221–24.
26. Some of the conversions credited to Antonia may have been "death bed" conversions, which were not rare at the time.
27. O'Brien, "Lady Antoinette Von Hoeffern," 221–24. There is confusion over the actual date of her death. O'Brien suggests that she did not live long after her return to Europe. However, other sources, such as the editorial notes to Baraga's diary, indicate that she outlived her brother and perished in 1871. See Walling and Rupp, *Diary of Bishop Frederic Baraga*, 31.
28. Ibid.
29. The prayer book and life of Christ may have been written in Ottawa—the sources are unclear.
30. Frederic Baraga to Frederick Rese, May 23, 1837, Clarke Historical Library, Bishop Baraga Collection.
31. Ibid.
32. Antonia was not the sister Baraga asked not to come to America previously—that was Amalia.
33. See Maureen Anna Harp, "Indian Missionaries, Immigrant Migrations, and Regional Catholic Culture: Slovene Missionaries in the Upper Great Lakes, 1830-1892" (PhD diss., University of Chicago, 1996), 94–95.
34. Ramsay Crooks to Lyman Warren, February 18, 1835, Clarke Historical Library, Bishop Baraga Collection. Also see the American Fur Company Papers at the Clarke Historical Library.
35. Frederic Baraga to Ramsay Crooks, February 25, 1836, Clarke Historical Library, Bishop Baraga Collection.
36. Loisson to Ramsay Crooks, October 5, 1837, Clarke Historical Library, Bishop Baraga Collection.
37. Ramsay Crooks to Frederic Baraga, May 5, 1838, Clarke Historical Library,

Bishop Baraga Collection. Crooks also told Baraga to expect some things that his sister sent, including blankets and a coffee pot.

38. Frederic Baraga to Ramsay Crooks, October 1, 1840, Clarke Historical Library, Bishop Baraga Collection.
39. Ramsay Crooks to Charles Borup, August 30, 1843, Clarke Historical Library, Bishop Baraga Collection.
40. Frederic Baraga to Peter Barbeau, March 6, 1852, Bayliss Public Library.
41. Catholic Native Americans to William Richmond, May 11, 1848, Clarke Historical Library, Bishop Baraga Collection. An editorial note on the transcription of the letter states that it was in Baraga's handwriting. Also see Russell M. Magnaghi, *Native Americans of Michigan's Upper Peninsula: A Chronology to 1900* (Marquette, MI: Center for Upper Peninsula Studies, 2009), 39; and Lambert, *Shepherd of the Wilderness*, 66.
42. Frederic Baraga to Bishop Lefevere, January 30, 1849, Clarke Historical Library, Bishop Baraga Collection. Baraga also mentioned in the letter that the Ojibwa language was "not so rich in words as the civilized languages." After all the years spent among Native Americans, he still felt them uncivilized, even when they converted and were literate.
43. The pope originally named Baraga as bishop of the apostolic vicariate. An actual diocese was not approved until 1857.
44. See Walling and Rupp, *Diary of Bishop Frederic Baraga*, 56–59; Murphy, "Frederic Baraga," 17. In the letter from Pope Pius IX to Baraga that informed him of his appointment, the pope told Baraga that he was chosen due to his "piety, zeal for religion, and missionary work among the Indians." The original name of the diocese was not Sault Sainte Marie and Marquette, however. Pius appointed Baraga "Bishop of Amyzonia." Pope Pius IX to Frederic Baraga, 29 July 29, 1853, Clarke Historical Library, Bishop Baraga Collection. In 1854 Baraga wrote Pius with the following request: "I . . . humbly petition that Your Holiness deign to erect my Vicariate to the status of a Diocese under the title of the Diocese of Mariopolis." He seemed embarrassed that four dioceses were named for the bishop's residences—Toronto, St. Paul, Milwaukee, and Detroit—while his was named for "a certain city in partibus infidelium" that surrounded him. Frederic Baraga to Pope Pius IX, March 5, 1854, Clarke Historical Library, Bishop Baraga Collection.
45. Frederic Baraga, "The Rt. Rev. Bishop Baraga's Report on the Missions of Lake Superior," *Detroit Catholic Vindicator* 1, no. 26 (October 22, 1853): 4.

46. Ibid. Also see Bernard Lambert, "Mission Priorities: Indians or Miners?" *Michigan History Magazine* 1967, 223–34.
47. Frederic Baraga to the Society of the Propagation of the Faith, December 30, 1853, Clarke Historical Library, Bishop Baraga Collection. Baraga felt his trip was a success overall, because he returned to the United States with a handful of priests in tow, as well as some seminarians who agreed to finish their training in the United States while working on their languages. Frederic Baraga to Archbishop J. Purcell of Cincinnati, May 15, 1854, Clarke Historical Library, Bishop Baraga Collection. By 1855 he had ordained four additional priests. For example, see *Detroit Catholic Vindicator* 3, no. 24 (1855), 2.
48. For example, see A. Lacoste to Frederic Baraga, August 1, 1855, Clarke Historical Library, Bishop Baraga Collection; Ignatius Mrak to Frederic Baraga, August 30, 1855, Clarke Historical Library, Bishop Baraga Collection; Frederic Baraga to George Manypenny, September 26, 1855, Clarke Historical Library, Bishop Baraga Collection.
49. Anonymous correspondent, "Episcopal Visitation," *Detroit Catholic Vindicator* 4, no. 20 (September 6, 1856), 2.
50. For example, see Frederic Baraga to the Leopoldine Foundation, June 23, 1859, Clarke Historical Library, Bishop Baraga Collection; and Frederic Baraga to the Leopoldine Foundation, September 8, 1859, Clarke Historical Library, Bishop Baraga Collection.
51. Frederic Baraga to the Society of the Propagation of the Faith, July 2, 1860, Clarke Historical Library, Bishop Baraga Collection.
52. Frederic Baraga to the Society of the Propagation of the Faith, February 4, 1862, Clarke Historical Library, Bishop Baraga Collection.
53. Edward Assinins to Frederic Baraga, September 3, 1865, Clarke Historical Library, Bishop Baraga Collection. Ultimately he had to let them down. He replied that it was too late in the season for him to travel, and that he would visit them the following summer. Frederic Baraga to Father Gerhard Terhort, October 1, 1865, Clarke Historical Library, Bishop Baraga Collection.
54. Frederic Baraga to Rev. Edward Jacker, December 11, 1865, Clarke Historical Library, Bishop Baraga Collection.
55. Frederic Baraga, Last Will and Testament, Marquette County Probate Court, January 4, 1866, Clarke Historical Library, Bishop Baraga Collection. An inventory of his property and assets appears in the appendix.
56. James Jamison, *By Cross and Anchor: The Story of Frederic Baraga on Lake*

Superior (Paterson, NJ: St. Anthony Guild Press, 1946), 175; Camier, "Frederic Baraga," 10. Also see Frederic Baraga to the Society of the Propagation of the Faith, January 30, 1867, Clarke Historical Library, Bishop Baraga Collection.

57. Frederic Baraga to Rev. J. O. Pare, February 1, 1867, Clarke Historical Library, Bishop Baraga Collection.
58. Frederic Baraga to Rev. P. B. Murray, February 19, 1867, Clarke Historical Library, Bishop Baraga Collection.
59. Rev. Edward Jacker to Rev. P. B. Murray, January 9, 1868, and January 19, 1868, Clarke Historical Library, Bishop Baraga Collection.
60. The best source of information on Ignatius Mrak comes from Antoine I. Rezek's *History of the Diocese of Sault Ste. Marie and Marquette,* 2 vols. (Chicago: M.A. Donohue and Co, 1906), 1:215–59.
61. Ibid., 218.
62. Ibid.
63. Ibid., 222–23.
64. Ibid., 230.
65. Stariha went to Minnesota in September 1871, and on October 28, 1902, he was consecrated bishop of the new diocese of Lead, South Dakota.
66. Rezek, *History of the Diocese of Sault Ste. Marie and Marquette,* 250–51.
67. Ibid., 246.
68. *Daily Mining Journal* (Marquette, MI), January 3, 1901.
69. *Daily Mining Journal* (Marquette, MI), January 5, 1901.
70. *Weekly Mining Journal* (Marquette, MI), January 26, 1901.
71. Unless otherwise noted, the information about Vertin in this section comes from Rezek, *History of the Diocese of Sault Ste. Marie and Marquette,* 260–323.
72. Marie Prisland, *From Slovenia—to America* (Chicago: Slovenian Women's Union of America, 1968), 90–91.
73. This would be approximately $300,000 in 2015.
74. Rezek, *History of the Diocese of Sault Ste. Marie and Marquette,* 265.
75. Rev. John Vertin to Father Bourion, May 28, 1879, quoted in Rezek, *History of the Diocese of Sault Ste. Marie and Marquette,* 265.
76. Rev. Kenny's move to Mackinac Island did not stop his parishioners from supporting him. According to Rezek, they referred to him as their "non-resident pastor" and sent him money and large shipments of food and clothing. See Ibid., 274.
77. This would be over $900,000 in 2015.

78. Rezek, *History of the Diocese of Sault Ste. Marie and Marquette*, 282–84.
79. Vertin left Mrak in charge of the diocese in his absence.
80. Rezek, *History of the Diocese of Sault Ste. Marie and Marquette*, 299, 303.
81. Rezek states that, "His circulars are permeated with admonitions to pastors to pray in common with their people, not only on Sundays but after the Mass on week-days." Ibid., 304.
82. Ibid., 316.
83. Once again, Mrak was left in charge in Vertin's absence.
84. Rezek, *History of the Diocese of Sault Ste. Marie and Marquette*, 321.
85. *Weekly Mining Journal* (Marquette, MI), March 4, 1899.
86. Ibid., 286.
87. *Weekly Mining Journal* (Marquette, MI), March 4, 1899.
88. *Daily Mining Journal* (Marquette, MI), January 5, 1901.
89. Mary Molek, ed., *Slovene Immigrant History, 1900–1950: Autobiographical Sketches by Ivan (John) Molek* (Dover, DE, 1979).
90. Ibid., 51.
91. Ibid., 52–53.
92. Ibid., 60.
93. Ibid., 58.
94. Ibid., 63–64.
95. Ibid., 65.
96. Ibid., 69.
97. Ibid., 71.
98. Ibid., 73.
99. Ibid., 74.
100. Ibid., 78–82.
101. Plautz noted that his father used a Germanized spelling of the name. See Frank Plautz, interview with Russell Magnaghi, n.d., Northern Michigan University and Area Audio Collection, Central Upper Peninsula and Northern Michigan University Archives.
102. Ibid. Also see Molek, *Slovene Immigrant History*, 68–69.
103. Plautz, interview.
104. Ibid.
105. Anna Murvich, interview, February 15, 1983, Northern Michigan University and Area Audio Collection, Central Upper Peninsula and Northern Michigan University Archives.

106. She also illustrates the frustration of researching Slovenes in Michigan by consistently referring to Slovenes as Austrians and then occasionally backtracking and correcting her oversight.
107. *Daily Mining Gazette* (Houghton, MI), August 13, 1982.
108. Angela S. Johnson, *Seasons of Faith: A Walk through the History of the Roman Catholic Diocese of Marquette, 1900–2000* (Marquette, MI: Roman Catholic Diocese of Marquette, 2006), 109–10.
109. Molek, *Slovene Immigrant History*, 76.
110. Anna Murvich recalled that the parish needed an organist, but could not find one, so a Slovene named Rady, who had attended a famous music school in Vienna, was brought in.
111. "Golden Jubilee Souvenir of the St. Joseph Church of Calumet," Michigan Technological University Archives, Houghton, MI.
112. *Diamond Jubilee 1965* (Calumet, MI: St. Joseph Calumet, 1965).
113. Ibid., 22.
114. Johnson, *Seasons of Faith*, 112.
115. This organization is listed in the Houghton County Articles of Association as the Slavonian Catholic St. Joseph Benevolent Society of Calumet. Its purpose was "Affording aid and relief to its numbers when in need. No person can become a member who is under 18 or over 55 or who belongs to any society which is forbidden by the Roman Catholic Church or is not free from all bodily disease. He must be a member of a Roman Catholic congregation and bear a good moral character and fulfill his duties generally as a Catholic Christian."
116. Prisland, *From Slovenia—to America*, 112.
117. Ibid., 42.
118. Plautz, interview.
119. See Houghton County Articles of Association.
120. "Golden Jubilee Souvenir of the St. Joseph Church of Calumet."
121. See "Mine Inspector's Report, Houghton County, Michigan," n.d., Michigan Technological University, Houghton, MI, 40–41.
122. Molek, *Slovene Immigrant History*, 73.
123. "1910 Census Stats Page," Northern Michigan University, http://www.nmu.edu/archives/1910-census-stats-page.
124. Plautz, interview.
125. Prisland, *From Slovenia—to America*, 115.
126. Untitled manuscript, St. John Vianney Highland Park Parish Collection, box 1,

folder 11, Archives of the Archdiocese of Detroit.

127. Ibid.

128. Ibid.

129. Rev. Bernard Ambrozic to Rt. Rev. M. Gallagher, April 2, 1926, St. John Vianney Highland Park Parish Collection, box 1, folder 4, Archives of the Archdiocese of Detroit.

130. Rev. Bernard Ambrozic to Rt. Rev. M. Gallagher, July 9, 1926, St. John Vianney Highland Park Parish Collection, box 1, folder 4, Archives of the Archdiocese of Detroit.

131. Rev. Bernard Ambrozic to Rt. Rev. M. Gallagher, September 23, 1926, St. John Vianney Highland Park Parish Collection, box 1, folder 4, Archives of the Archdiocese of Detroit.

132. Rev. Kazimir Zakrajsek to Rt. Rev. M. Gallagher, September 20, 1926, St. John Vianney Highland Park Parish Collection, box 1, folder 4, Archives of the Archdiocese of Detroit.

133. Rt. Rev. M. Gallagher to Rev. Kazimir Zakrajsek, September 28, 1926, St. John Vianney Highland Park Parish Collection, box 1, folder 4, Archives of the Archdiocese of Detroit.

134. Rev. Bernard Ambrozic to Rt. Rev. Michael Gallagher, November 16, 1930, St. John Vianney Highland Park Parish Collection, box 1, folder 4, Archives of the Archdiocese of Detroit.

135. Ibid.

136. Church Committee of St. John Vianney to Rt. Rev. Michael Gallagher, November 22, 1930, St. John Vianney Highland Park Parish Collection, box 1, folder 4, Archives of the Archdiocese of Detroit.

137. Rt. Rev. Michael Gallagher to Rev. Bernard Ambrozic, November 24, 1930, St. John Vianney Highland Park Parish Collection, box 1, folder 4, Archives of the Archdiocese of Detroit. According to the Silver Jubilee Souvenir Program of St. John Vianney, published in 1952, Esser stayed until 1931, when Rev. Odilo Hajnsek, another Franciscan, replaced him. See box 1, folder 11, St. John Vianney Highland Park Parish Collection, Archives of the Archdiocese of Detroit.

138. "New Structure for Slovenians to Be Blessed," *Michigan Catholic* 1933, St. John Vianney Highland Park Parish Collection, box 1, folder 11, Archives of the Archdiocese of Detroit.

139. Rev. Augustine Svete to Chancery Office, May 18, 1937, St. John Vianney Highland Park Parish Collection, box 1, folder 5, Archives of the Archdiocese of De-

troit.

140. St. John Vianney Church to Rt. Rev. Edward Mooney, October 14, 1942, St. John Vianney Highland Park Parish Collection, box 1, folder 6, Archives of the Archdiocese of Detroit; Chancellor Hickey to Rev. Augustine Svete, October 17, 1942, St. John Vianney Highland Park Parish Collection, box 1, folder 6, Archives of the Archdiocese of Detroit.
141. *Official Report 1940*, St. John Vianney Highland Park Parish Collection, box 1, folder 12, Archives of the Archdiocese of Detroit.
142. *Official Report 1948*, St. John Vianney Highland Park Parish Collection, box 1, folder 11, Archives of the Archdiocese of Detroit.
143. Vice Chancellor to Rev. Thomas Hoge, February 27, 1951, St. John Vianney Highland Park Parish Collection, box 1, folder 1, Archives of the Archdiocese of Detroit. The new boundaries were the middle of McNichols Road to the north, the middle of Hamilton Avenue to the east, the middle of Puritan Avenue to the south, and Baylis Avenue to the west.
144. Untitled manuscript, St. John Vianney Highland Park Parish Collection, box 1, folder 11, Archives of the Archdiocese of Detroit.
145. *1977 Official Report*, St. John Vianney Highland Park Parish Collection, box 1, folder 8, Archives of the Archdiocese of Detroit.
146. Father Athanasius Lovrencic to Rt. Rev. John Dearden, June 30, 1978, St. John Vianney Highland Park Parish Collection, box 1, folder 9, Archives of the Archdiocese of Detroit.
147. Valerie Holland to Rt. Rev. John Dearden, n.d., St. John Vianney Highland Park Parish Collection, box 1, folder 9, Archives of the Archdiocese of Detroit. A response from Assistant Bishop Joseph Imesch assured Holland that the reason that the church had to close was the lack of priests and the fact that St. John Vianney only had approximately fifty families. See Bishop Joseph Imesch to Valerie Holland, August 30, 1978, St. John Vianney Highland Park Parish Collection, box 1, folder 9, Archives of the Archdiocese of Detroit.
148. Archbishop John Cardinal Dearden, Decree to Suppress St. John Vianney, September 26, 1978, St. John Vianney Highland Park Parish Collection, box 1, folder 1, Archives of the Archdiocese of Detroit.
149. James M. Anderson, ed., *Ethnic Groups in Michigan* (Detroit: Ethnos Press, 1983).
150. See Daniel Cetinich, *South Slavs in Michigan* (East Lansing: Michigan State University Press, 2003), 66; and George J. Prpic, *South Slavic Immigration in*

America (Boston: Twayne Publishers, 1978), 147.

151. *Daily Mining Gazette* (Houghton, MI), March 28, 1985.
152. Loret Ruppe Vertical File, Michigan Technological University Archives, Houghton, MI; *Detroit News*, June 12, 1988.
153. Edward Gobetz, *Slovenian Heritage, Volume I* (Willoughby Hills, OH: Slovenian Research Center of America, 1980), 130.
154. Harp, "Indian Missionaries, Immigrant Migrations, and Regional Catholic Culture," 25–26.
155. For more on Pierz and Buh, see Harp's dissertation; also see Bernard Coleman and Verona LaBud, *Masinaigans: The Little Book; A Biography of Monsignor Joseph F. Buh, Slovenian Missionary in America, 1864–1922* (St. Paul, MN: North Central Publishing Co., 1972); and A. J. Rezek, *The History of the Diocese of Sault Ste. Marie and Marquette* (Chicago: M.A. Donohue and Co., 1906). Rezek, *History of the Diocese of Sault Ste. Marie and Marquette*, also provides biographical information on Skolla.
156. See Joseph Gregorich, "Contributions of the Slovenes to the Chippewa and Ottawa Indian Missions," *Michigan History Magazine*, 1967, 168–83.
157. There is a long history of Protestants who have said that Catholics convert and baptize too many Native Americans without any thought. For example, Roger Williams wrote a famous diatribe against the Catholics on this issue. See Williams, *Christenings Make Not Christians*, ed. Perry Miller (New York, 1964), 26–41.
158. "Bishop Baraga Association," Roman Catholic Diocese of Marquette, www.dioceseofmarquette.org/bishopbaragaassociation.

For Further Reference

Baraga, Frederic. *Admonition for the Holy Year*. Ljubljana, Yugoslavia: Brat Francisek, 1826.

———. *Apostolic Letter about the Immaculate Conception of Virgin Mary*. Ljubljana, Yugoslavia: Brat Francisek, 1865.

———. *Answers to the Inquiries Respecting the History, Present Condition, and Future Prospects of the Indian Tribes of the United States*. New York: Studia Slovenica, 1976.

———. "Lecture on the Indians, Their Manners and Customs and Their Way of Living, 1863." *Acta et Dicta* 5, no. 1 (1917): 102–10.

Bodnar, John. *The Transplanted: A History of Immigrants in Urban America*. Bloomington: Indiana University Press, 1985.

Camier, Walter Thomas. "Frederic Baraga: The Snowshoe Priest." *Crusade*, May/June, 2000, 9–16.

Canfield, Frances X. "A Diocese So Vast: Bishop Rese in Detroit." *Michigan History Magazine*, 1967, 202–11.

Cetinich, Daniel. *South Slavs in Michigan*. East Lansing: Michigan State University Press, 2003.

Cleland, Charles. *Rites of Conquest: The History and Culture of Michigan's Native Americans*. Ann Arbor: University of Michigan Press, 1992.

Coleman, Bernard, and Verona LaBud. *Masinaigans: The Little Book; A Biography of Monsignor Joseph F. Buh, Slovenian Missionary in America, 1864–1922*. St. Paul, MN: North Central Publishing Co., 1972.

Danziger, Edmund Jefferson. *The Chippewas of Lake Superior*. Norman: University of Oklahoma Press, 1990.

———. *Great Lakes Indian Accommodation and Resistance during the Early Reservation Years, 1850–1900*. Ann Arbor: University of Michigan Press, 2009.

Delene, Elizabeth. "Bishop Frederic Baraga." *Harlow's Wooden Man* Fall 1997, 3–10.

Demaray, Agnes. "The Shrine of the Snowshoe Priest." *Lake Superior Port Cities Magazine*, 1984, 1–16.

Dunbar, Willis F. *Michigan: A History of the Wolverine State*. Grand Rapids, MI: William B. Eerdmans Publishing Company, 1980.

Elliott, Richard R. "Apostolate of Father Baraga among the Chippewas and Whites of Lake Superior." *American Catholic Quarterly Review* 21 (1896): 596–617.

———. "Chippewas of Lake Superior." *American Catholic Quarterly Review* 21 (1896): 354–73.

———. "Chippewas and Ottawas: Father Baraga's Books in Their Language." *American Catholic Quarterly Review* 22 (1897): 18–46.

———. "Frederic Baraga among the Ottawa." *American Catholic Quarterly Review* 21 (1896): 106–29.

Elliott, Walter. "Bishop Baraga—The Apostle of the Chippewas." *Catholic World* 73 (1901): 78–87.

Gobetz, Edward. *Slovenian Heritage, Volume I*. Willoughby Hills, OH: Slovenian Research Center of America, 1980.

Gregorich, Joseph. "Contributions of the Slovenes to the Chippewa and Ottawa Indian Missions." *Michigan History Magazine*, 1967, 168–83.

———. *The Apostle of the Chippewas: The Life Story of the Most Rev. Frederick Baraga, D.D., the First Bishop of Marquette*. Chicago: Bishop Baraga Association, 1932.

Haas, Francis J. *Frederic Baraga: Adventurer for Christ*. Marquette, MI: Cause of Bishop Baraga, 1950.

Handlin, Oscar. *The Uprooted: The Epic Story of the Great Migrations That Made the American People*. Boston: Little, Brown, and Company, 1951.

Jacker, Edward. "Life and Services of Bishop Baraga." Lecture delivered in Marquette, MI. January 30, 1868.

Jamison, James. *By Cross and Anchor: The Story of Frederic Baraga on Lake Superior*.

Paterson, NJ: St. Anthony Guild Press, 1946.

Jezernik, Maksimilijan. *Frederick Baraga.* New York: Studia Slovenica, 1968.

Lambert, Bernard. "Mission Priorities: Indians or Miners?" *Michigan History Magazine,*1967, 223–34.

———. *Shepherd of the Wilderness: A Biography of Bishop Frederic Baraga.* Hancock, MI: Book Concern Printers, 1967.

MacDonald, Graham A., trans. and ed. *Frederic Baraga's Short History of the North American Indians.* Calgary: University of Calgary Press, 2004.

Magnaghi, Russell M. *A Guide to the Indians of Michigan's Upper Peninsula, 1621–1900.* Marquette, MI: Belle Fontaine Press, 1984.

———. *The Way It Happened: Settling Michigan's Upper Peninsula.* Iron Mountain, MI: Mid-Peninsula Library Cooperative, 1982.

Molek, Mary, ed., *Slovene Immigrant History 1900–1950: Autobiographical Sketches by Ivan (John) Molek.* Dover, DE, 1979.

Parton, James. "Our Roman Catholic Brethren." *Atlantic Monthly,* April 1868, 432–51.

Peters, Bernard C. "Hypocrisy on the Great Lakes Frontier: The Use of Whiskey by the Michigan Department of Indian Affairs." *Michigan Historical Review* 18, no. 2 (Fall 1992): 1–13.

———. "Whiskey Traffic on Lake Superior: Who Brought the Whiskey to L'Anse in 1843?" *Inland Seas* 58, no. 2 (Summer 2002): 104–18.

Pitezel, John H. *Lights and Shades of Missionary Life: Containing Travels, Sketches, Incidents, and Missionary Efforts, during Nine Years Spent in the Region of Lake Superior.* Cincinnati, OH, 1859.

Prisland, Marie. *From Slovenia—to America.* Chicago: Slovenian Women's Union of America, 1968.

Prpic, George. *South Slavic Immigration in America.* Boston: Twayne Publishers, 1978.

Rezek, Antoine I. *History of the Diocese of Sault Ste. Marie and Marquette.* 2 vols. Chicago: M.A. Donohue and Co, 1906.

Susel, Rudolph M. "Slovenes." In *Harvard Encyclopedia of American Ethnic Groups,* ed. Stephan Thernstrom, Ann Orlov, and Oscar Handlin. Cambridge, MA: Harvard University Press, 1980.

Verwyst, Chrysostomus P. *Life and Labors of Rt. Rev. Frederic Baraga, First Bishop of Marquette, Mich.* Milwaukee, WI: M.S. Wiltzius & Co., 1900.

Washburn, Wilcomb, ed. *The American Indian and the United States: A Documentary*

History. 4 vols. New York: Random House, 1973.

Walling, Regis, and N. Daniel Rupp, eds. *The Diary of Bishop Frederic Baraga: First Bishop of Marquette, Michigan*. Translated by Joseph Gregorich and Paul Prud'homme. Detroit: Wayne State University Press, 1990.

Index